CHE

CHE
A memoir by Fidel Castro

Edited by David Deutschmann

Preface by Jesús Montané

OCEAN

Cover design by David Spratt

ISBN paper 1-875284-15-X

First edition, 1994

Printed in Australia

Published by Ocean Press,
GPO Box 3279, Melbourne, Victoria 3001, Australia

Distributed in the USA by The Talman Company,
131 Spring Street, New York, NY 10012, USA
Distributed in Britain and Europe by Central Books,
99 Wallis Road, London E9 5LN, Britain
Distributed in Australia by Astam Books,
57-71 John Street, Leichhardt, NSW 2040, Australia
Distributed in Cuba by Ocean Press,
Apartado 686, C.P. 11300, Havana, Cuba

Contents

Acknowledgements

Ernesto Che Guevara   **1**

Fidel Castro   **3**

Chronology   **5**

Preface *by Jesús Montané*   **11**

Introduction *by David Deutschmann*   **22**

Chapter one   **32**

Chapter two   **38**

Chapter three   **68**

Chapter four   **80**

Chapter five   **97**

Chapter six   **112**

Chapter seven   **134**

Postscript   **159**

Glossary   **162**

Acknowledgments

The editor and publisher wish to acknowledge the assistance of the following in preparing this book for publication: Jesús Montané for his constant encouragement of the project; Pedro Alvarez Tabio of the Office of Publications of the Council of State for providing several previously unpublished photos; the late Osvaldo Salas for once again making available his photo archives; Mario Mencía for assisting with the chronology; and the Cuban Institute for Friendship with the Peoples for their support over the years.

Ernesto Che Guevara

Ernesto Guevara de la Serna was born in Rosario, Argentina on June 14, 1928. As a medical student in Buenos Aires and after earning his degree as doctor, he traveled throughout Latin America. Living in Guatemala during 1954 — then under the elected government of Jacobo Arbenz — he became involved in political activity there and was an eyewitness to the overthrow of that government in a CIA-organized military operation.

Forced to leave Guatemala under threat of death, Guevara went to Mexico City. There he linked up with exiled Cuban revolutionaries seeking to overthrow dictator Fulgencio Batista. In July 1955 he met Fidel Castro and immediately enlisted in the guerrilla expedition Castro was organizing. The Cubans nicknamed him "Che," a popular form of address in Argentina.

From November 25 to December 2, 1956, Guevara was part of the expedition that sailed to Cuba aboard the cabin cruiser *Granma* to begin the revolutionary armed struggle in the Sierra Maestra mountains. Originally the troop doctor, he became the first Rebel Army commander in July 1957.

In September 1958, Guevara and Camilo Cienfuegos each led guerrilla columns westward from the Sierra Maestra to the center of the island. Through fierce fighting they successfully extended the Rebel Army's operations to much of Cuba. At the end of December 1958, Guevara led the Rebel Army forces to victory in the battle of Santa Clara, one of the decisive engagements of the war.

Following the rebels' victory on January 1, 1959, Guevara became a key leader of the new revolutionary government. In September 1959 he began serving as head of the Department of Industry of the National Institute of Agrarian Reform; in November 1959 he became president of the National Bank; and in February 1961 he became minister of industry. He was also a central leader of the political organization that in 1965 became the Communist Party of Cuba.

Guevara was a leading Cuban representative around the world, heading numerous delegations and speaking at the United Nations and other international forums.

In April 1965 Guevara left Cuba to participate directly in revolutionary struggles abroad. He spent several months in the Congo in Africa, returning to Cuba secretly in December 1965. In November 1966 he arrived in Bolivia, where he led a guerrilla detachment fighting that country's military dictatorship. Wounded and captured by U.S.-trained Bolivian counter-insurgency troops on October 8, 1967, he was murdered the following day.

Fidel Castro

Fidel Castro Ruz was born in Birán, in the former province of Oriente, on August 13, 1926. Born into a well-off landowning family, he received his primary education in a rural school, later attended private Jesuit schools in Santiago de Cuba and Havana, and graduated from law school at the University of Havana.

While at the university, he joined a student group against political corruption. He was a member of the Cuban People's Party (also known as the Orthodox Party) in 1947 and became a leader of its left wing. That same year, he volunteered for an armed expedition against the Trujillo dictatorship in the Dominican Republic (the expeditionaries were unable to leave Cuba to carry out their plans). As a student leader, Castro was in Colombia to help organize a Latin American anti-imperialist student congress and participated in the April 1948 popular uprising in Bogotá.

After Fulgencio Batista's coup d'état of March 10, 1952, Castro began to organize a revolutionary organization to initiate armed insurrection against the U.S.-backed Batista dictatorship. He organized and led an unsuccessful attack on the Moncada army garrison in Santiago de Cuba on July 26, 1953, for which he and over two dozen others were captured, tried, found guilty, and imprisoned; more than 60 revolutionaries were murdered by Batista's army during and immediately after the Moncada attack. While in prison Castro edited his defense speech from the trial into the pamphlet *History will absolve me*, which was distributed in tens of thousands of copies and became the program of what was to become the July 26 Movement. Originally sentenced to 15 years, he and his comrades were released from prison 22 months later in May 1955 as a result of a growing public campaign.

On July 7, 1955, Castro left for Mexico, where he began to organize a guerrilla expedition to Cuba to launch the armed insurrection. On December 2, 1956, along with 81 other fighters, including his brother Raúl, Che Guevara, Camilo Cienfuegos, Juan

Almeida and Jesús Montané, Castro reached the Cuban coast aboard the cabin cruiser *Granma*. For the next two years, Castro directed the operations of the Rebel Army, in addition to continuing as central leader of the July 26 Movement. After an initial setback, the guerrillas were able to reorganize their forces and by late 1958 had successfully extended the struggle from the Sierra Maestra mountains to the heart of the island.

On January 1, 1959, Batista fled Cuba. In response to a call by Castro, hundreds of thousands of Cubans launched an insurrectionary general strike that ensured the victory of the revolution. Castro arrived triumphantly in Havana on January 8 as commander in chief of Cuba's victorious Rebel Army. On February 13, 1959, he was named prime minister, a position he held until December 1976, when he became president of the Council of State and the Council of Ministers.

He has been first secretary of the Central Committee of the Communist Party since its founding in 1965.

Chronology

June 14, 1928 Ernesto Guevara is born in Rosario, Argentina, of parents Ernesto Guevara Lynch and Celia de la Serna.

1945-51 Guevara is enrolled at medical school in Buenos Aires.

January-July 1952 Guevara visits Peru, Colombia, and Venezuela. While in Peru he works in a leper colony treating patients.

March 10, 1952 Fulgencio Batista carries out coup d'etat in Cuba.

March 1953 Guevara graduates as a doctor.

July 6, 1953 After graduating, Guevara travels throughout Latin America. He visits Bolivia, observing the impact of the 1952 revolution.

July 26, 1953 Fidel Castro leads an armed attack on the Moncada army garrison in Santiago de Cuba, launching the revolutionary struggle to overthrow the Batista regime. The attack fails and Batista's troops massacre more than 50 captured combatants. Castro and other survivors are soon captured and imprisoned.

December 1953 Guevara has first contact with a group of survivors of the Moncada attack in San José, Costa Rica.

December 24, 1953 Guevara arrives in Guatemala, then under the elected government of Jacobo Arbenz.

January 4, 1954 Guevara meets Ñico López, a veteran of the Moncada attack, in Guatemala City.

January-June 1954 Unable to find a medical position in Guatemala, Guevara obtains various odd jobs. He studies Marxism and becomes involved in political activities, meeting exiled Cuban revolutionaries.

June 17, 1954 Mercenary forces backed by the CIA invade Guatemala. Guevara volunteers to fight.

June 27, 1954 Arbenz resigns.

September 21, 1954   Guevara arrives in Mexico City after fleeing Guatemala.

May 15, 1955   Fidel Castro and other Moncada survivors are freed from prison in Cuba due to a massive public campaign in defense of their civil rights.

June 1955   Guevara encounters Ñico López, who is also in Mexico City. Several days later López arranges a meeting for him with Raúl Castro.

July 7, 1955   Fidel Castro arrives in Mexico with the goal of organizing an armed expedition to Cuba.

July 1955   Guevara meets Fidel Castro and immediately enrolls as the third confirmed member of the future guerrilla expedition. Guevara subsequently becomes involved in training combatants, with the Cubans giving him the nickname "Che," an Argentinian term of greeting.

November 25, 1956   Eighty-two combatants, including Guevara as doctor, sail for Cuba aboard the small cabin cruiser *Granma*, leaving from Tuxpan in Mexico.

December 2, 1956   *Granma* reaches Cuba at Las Coloradas beach in Oriente Province. The rebel combatants are surprised by Batista's troops and dispersed. A majority of the guerrillas are either murdered or captured; Guevara is wounded.

December 21, 1956   Guevara's group reunites with Fidel Castro; at this point there are 15 fighters in the Rebel Army.

January 17, 1957   Rebel Army overruns an army outpost in the battle of La Plata.

May 27-28, 1957   Battle of El Uvero takes place in the Sierra Maestra, with a major victory for the Rebel Army as it captures a well-fortified army garrison.

July 1957   Rebel Army organizes a second column. Guevara is selected to lead it and is promoted to the rank of commander.

May 24, 1958   Batista launches an all-out military offensive against the Rebel Army in the Sierra Maestra. The offensive eventually fails.

August 31, 1958   Guevara leads an invasion column from the Sierra Maestra toward Las Villas Province in central Cuba, and days later signs the Pedrero Pact with the March 13 Revolutionary Directorate, which had a strong guerrilla base there.

Several days earlier Camilo Cienfuegos had been ordered to lead another column toward Pinar del Río Province on the western end of Cuba.

October 16, 1958 The Rebel Army column led by Guevara arrives in the Escambray Mountains.

December 1958 Rebel columns of Guevara and the March 13 Revolutionary Directorate, and Cienfuegos with a small guerrilla troop of the Popular Socialist Party, capture a number of towns in Las Villas Province and effectively cut the island in half.

December 28, 1958 Guevara's column begins the battle of Santa Clara, the capital of Las Villas.

January 1, 1959 Batista flees Cuba. A military junta takes over. Fidel Castro opposes the new junta and calls for the revolutionary struggle to continue. Santa Clara falls to the Rebel Army. Guevara and Cienfuegos are ordered immediately to Havana.

January 2, 1959 Cuban workers respond to Fidel Castro's call for a general strike and the country is paralyzed. The Rebel Army columns of Guevara and Cienfuegos arrive in Havana.

January 8, 1959 Fidel Castro arrives in Havana, greeted by hundreds of thousands of people.

February 9, 1959 Guevara is declared a Cuban citizen in recognition of his contribution to Cuba's liberation.

February 16, 1959 Fidel Castro becomes prime minister.

May 17, 1959 Proclamation of the first agrarian reform law, fixing legal holdings at a maximum of 1,000 acres and distributing land to peasants.

October 7, 1959 Guevara is designated head of the Department of Industry of the National Institute of Agrarian Reform (INRA).

October 21, 1959 Following an attempt to initiate a counter-revolutionary uprising, Huber Matos, military commander of Camagüey Province, is arrested by army chief of staff Camilo Cienfuegos.

October 28, 1959 Camilo Cienfuegos's plane goes down over sea. Cienfuegos is lost at sea.

November 26, 1959 Guevara is appointed president of the National Bank of Cuba.

July-October 1960   Cuba nationalizes all major foreign and domestic industries and banks.

April 17-19, 1961   1,500 Cuban-born mercenaries, organized and backed by the United States, invade Cuba at the Bay of Pigs on the southern coast. The aim was to establish a "provisional government" to appeal for direct U.S. intervention. They are defeated within 72 hours, with the last ones surrendering at Playa Girón (Girón Beach), which has come to be the name used by the Cubans for the battle. Guevara is sent to command troops in Pinar del Río Province.

October 22, 1962   President Kennedy initiates the "Cuban Missile Crisis," denouncing Cuba's acquisition of missiles capable of carrying nuclear warheads for defense against U.S. attack. Washington imposes a naval blockade on Cuba. Cuba responds by mobilizing its population for defense. Guevara is assigned to lead forces in Pinar del Río Province in preparation for an imminent U.S. invasion.

October 28, 1962   Soviet Premier Khrushchev agrees to remove Soviet missiles in exchange for U.S. pledge not to invade Cuba.

March 1964   Guevara meets with Tamara Bunke (Tania) and discusses her mission to move to Bolivia in anticipation of a future guerrilla expedition.

December 9, 1964   Guevara leaves Cuba on a three-month state visit, speaking at the United Nations. He then visits a number of African countries.

March 14, 1965   Guevara returns to Cuba and shortly afterwards drops from public view.

April 1, 1965   Guevara delivers a farewell letter to Fidel Castro. He subsequently leaves Cuba on an internationalist mission in the Congo (now Zaire), entering through Tanzania. Guevara operates under the name Tatú, Swahili for "number two."

April 18, 1965   In answer to questions about Guevara's whereabouts, Castro tells foreign reporters that Guevara "will always be where he is most useful to the revolution."

June 16, 1965   Castro announces Guevara's whereabouts will be revealed "when Commander Guevara wants it known."

October 3, 1965   Castro publicly reads Guevara's letter of farewell at a meeting to announce the Central Committee of the newly-formed Communist Party of Cuba.

December 1965 Castro arranges for Guevara to return to Cuba in secret. Guevara prepares for an expedition to Bolivia.

January 3-14, 1966 Tricontinental Conference of Solidarity of the Peoples of Asia, Africa, and Latin America is held in Havana.

March 1966 Arrival in Bolivia of the first Cuban combatants to begin advance preparations for a guerrilla detachment.

July 1966 Guevara meets with Cuban volunteers selected for the mission to Bolivia at a training camp in Cuba's Pinar del Río Province.

November 4, 1966 Guevara arrives in Bolivia in disguise and using an assumed name.

November 7, 1966 Guevara arrives at site where Bolivian guerrilla movement will be based; first entry in Bolivian diary.

November-December 1966 More guerrilla combatants arrive and base camps are established.

December 31, 1966 Guevara meets with Bolivian Communist Party secretary Mario Monje. There is disagreement over perspectives for the planned guerrilla expedition.

February 1-March 20, 1967 Guerrilla detachment leaves the base camp to explore the region.

March 23, 1967 First guerrilla military action takes place with combatants successfully ambushing a Bolivian army column.

April 10, 1967 Guerrilla column conducts a successful ambush of Bolivian troops.

April 16, 1967 Publication of Guevara's Message to the Tricontinental with his call for the creation of "two, three, many Vietnams."

April 17, 1967 Guerrilla detachment led by Joaquín is separated from the rest of the unit. The separation is supposed to last only three days but the two groups are unable to reunite.

April 20, 1967 Régis Debray is arrested after having spent several weeks with a guerrilla unit. He is subsequently tried and sentenced to 30 years imprisonment.

May 1967 U.S. Special Forces arrive in Bolivia to train counter-insurgency troops of the Bolivian army.

July 6, 1967 Guerrillas occupy the town of Samaipata.

July 26, 1967 Guevara gives a speech to guerrillas on the significance of the July 26, 1953, attack on the Moncada garrison.

July 31-August 10, 1967 Organization of Latin American Solidarity (OLAS) conference is held in Havana. The conference supports guerrilla movements throughout Latin America. Che Guevara is elected honorary chair.

August 4, 1967 Deserter leads the Bolivian army to the guerrillas' main supply cache; documents seized lead to arrest of key urban contacts.

August 31, 1967 Joaquín's detachment is ambushed and annihilated while crossing a river after an informer leads government troops to the site.

September 26, 1967 Guerrillas walk into an ambush. Three are killed and government forces encircle the remaining guerrilla forces.

October 8, 1967 Remaining 17 guerrillas are trapped by Bolivian troops and conduct a desperate battle. Guevara is seriously wounded and captured.

October 9, 1967 Guevara and two other captured guerrillas are murdered following instructions from the Bolivian government and Washington.

October 15, 1967 In a television appearance Fidel Castro confirms news of Guevara's death and declares three days of official mourning in Cuba. October 8 is designated Day of the Heroic Guerrilla.

October 18, 1967 Castro delivers memorial speech for Guevara in Havana's Revolution Plaza before an audience of almost one million people.

February 22, 1968 Three Cuban survivors cross border into Chile, after having traveled across the Andes on foot to elude Bolivian army. They later return to Cuba.

Mid-March 1968 Microfilm of Guevara's Bolivian diary arrives in Cuba.

July 1, 1968 Guevara's Bolivian diary published in Cuba and distributed free of charge to the Cuban people. The introduction is by Fidel Castro.

Preface

by Jesús Montané Oropesa

When Fidel Castro left Havana for exile in Mexico on Thursday, July 7, 1955, because his life was in danger in Cuba, he was about to meet Che.

The group of survivors of the July 26, 1953, attack on the Moncada garrison — an action with which we had tried to initiate a people's armed insurrection — had been confined in the prison on the Isle of Pines until our release 53 days earlier, on Sunday, May 15.

During those 53 days, in which Fidel had remained in Havana, he waged a daring, dangerous political battle through some of the mass media. He denounced the crimes the Batista dictatorship had committed against those who had attacked the Moncada and Bayamo garrisons, the abuses against those who opposed the oppressive system, the exploitation by which the workers were victimized and the lack of guarantees for peaceful political struggle. He challenged the government to hold a general election immediately. His main aim was to force the dictator Fulgencio Batista to show what lay behind his demagogic statements about a democratic opening in the country.

All of that activity was in line with a very carefully planned tactic to force the dictatorship to reveal its despotic, criminal nature. It would also show that even our freedom wasn't due to any kindly gesture by the regime. The government had been forced to free us because of a nationwide campaign calling for amnesty for political prisoners.

Not all of the political forces saw the situation so clearly, however, and not all of them really intended to pay whatever

11

price might be required to solve the prevailing crisis. Former President Carlos Prío Socarrás, who had been overthrown, was preparing to return to Cuba; this implied his renunciation of the use of arms and his craven acceptance of the rules Batista had imposed for a "normalization" that, in practice, would amount to the indefinite prolongation of his stay in power. One way or another and for various reasons, the other opposition political parties were also moving toward that line of negotiations that would never lead to a positive solution of the problem.

That was the situation in which Fidel waged that tactical-political battle. The result was a foregone conclusion, as he knew that the dictatorship wasn't about to allow any real opposition to exist. One by one, all possibilities of normal political struggle were closed off. The police began to harass and arrest some of his closest followers. His brother Raúl was falsely accused of having engaged in terrorism and had to go into exile. Fidel's phone was tapped; he received anonymous death threats; he was kept from participating in mass meetings; radio and television programs in which he was to participate were cancelled; and finally, the daily *La Calle*, the only paper in which he could air his views, was shut down.

He had foreseen this, so while conducting the public political battle right from the day we got out of prison, he also dedicated himself to another, secret task: that of creating the July 26 Revolutionary Movement (MR-26-7), a solid underground organization that would bring together the most radical sectors of young people from all over the country to begin a people's armed insurrection. The July 26 Revolutionary Movement's function would be to organize, train and arm the people for that confrontation while a small armed contingent was formed and trained outside Cuba to return, initiate and lead the revolutionary war.

Those were the special circumstances in which Fidel reached Mexico in the first week of July 1955. In that same month, he met the young Argentinian doctor Ernesto Guevara de la Serna, whom the few Cubans who knew him were already calling Che.

Coming from Guatemala, Che had reached Mexico on September 21, 1954. He had completed his medical studies at the University of Buenos Aires on April 11, 1953. On June 12, he received his diploma as a doctor, and on July 6 he left the Argentinian capital and his country, never to return. The day on which we attacked the Moncada garrison [July 26, 1953], Che happened to be in Bolivia, where, 14 years later, he was to die heroically, once more setting an impressive example as a true internationalist.

In the middle of December 1953, Che had his first, chance contact with several Cubans who had taken part in the July 26 actions. They had gone into exile and were living in San José, Costa Rica. But Che really developed an ideological affinity with the Cuban revolution while in Guatemala City from January 3, 1954, when he met Antonio "Ñico" López.

After taking part in the attack on the Bayamo military garrison — an operation supporting the attack on the Moncada garrison — Ñico López managed to escape and obtained political asylum in Guatemala. Over 6 feet tall and extremely thin, that 21-year-old was one of our best-loved comrades. Since he came from a very low-income family, Ñico hadn't been able to study very much, but he was one of Fidel's young followers who had the most radical thinking; he was also very dynamic and brave. He worked sporadically as a porter in a food market in Havana and turned his hand to many other things to support himself and his family.

Ñico was the first person who talked to Che about our revolutionary movement and about the armed actions that the young lawyer Fidel Castro had led in Cuba. Ñico and Che began an exemplary friendship in Guatemala which was strengthened in Mexico and ended only with Ñico's death on December 8, 1956, after the cabin cruiser *Granma* had taken us to Oriente Province.

When Jacobo Arbenz's democratic, nationalist administration was overthrown in Guatemala, Che went to Mexico. Ten months later, he met Fidel there in the home of María Antonia González, a Cuban emigre, in circumstances which he himself described:

From there [Guatemala], I escaped to Mexico when FBI agents were arresting and killing everybody who might constitute a threat to the United Fruit Company's government. In Mexico, I saw some members of the July 26 Movement whom I'd met in Guatemala, and I became friends with Raúl Castro, Fidel's younger brother. He introduced me to the head of the Movement when they were already planning the invasion of Cuba.

I talked with Fidel all night. By the time the sun came up, I was the doctor of his future expedition. In fact, after the experiences I'd had during my long trek through Latin America and its finale in Guatemala, I didn't need much persuading to join any revolution against a tyrant, but Fidel impressed me as an extraordinary man. He tackled and did the impossible things. He had exceptional faith that, once he left for Cuba, he would get there; once he got there, he would fight; and, by fighting, he would win. I shared his optimism. It was necessary to take action, struggle, make things happen, stop crying and fight. And, to show the people of his home-land that they could believe in him, because he did what he said, he launched his famous "In '56, we will be free or martyrs" and announced that before the end of the year, he would land somewhere in Cuba at the head of his expeditionary army. [Excerpt from Jorge Ricardo Masetti's April 1958 interview of Che in the Sierra Maestra. It appears in Masetti's book *Los que luchan y los que lloran (El Fidel Castro que yo vi)* [Those who fight and those who cry (The Fidel Castro I saw)], Editorial Madiedo, Havana, 1960]

Che had turned 27 on June 14, 1955, a month before that meeting; Fidel would turn 29 a few days later, on August 13. They were of the same generation, but their practical-ideological identity, which would grow ever deeper with the passing time, was more important than that coincidence in linking them.

Che didn't write very much about that period, but a comparison of what little he did write with Fidel's documents of that period provides the key to the fellow feeling that immediately sprang up between them.

During those early days after their meeting, Fidel wrote as follows to those of us in the national leadership of the Movement who remained in Havana:

The norm governing my actions here is and will always be extreme care and absolute discretion, as if we were in Cuba. I've managed to keep a very low profile. As you advance there, we will advance here. I think that everything can be done perfectly well, as outlined.

That's why I didn't make any public statements on arrival. A sense of propriety also kept me from doing so. Nobody has the right to cry about Cuba's troubles anywhere in the world as long as there is a Cuban who can take up a rifle to remedy them. If we were to talk to the Mexicans about our shameful political situation, they might ask us what the Cubans are doing about it. As if they had few problems themselves! If worst comes to worst, it may be said of us in the future that we gave our lives trying to do something impossible — but never that we cried from impotence.

Don't those statements of Fidel's, made on July 14, 1955, express the same personality and temperament that we later discovered were Che's too? On August 2 of that same year, in another letter, Fidel wrote:

I think that I'm carrying out my task fully. In this case, I'm referring not to writing letters and manifestos from this isolated little room but rather to another, no less important task. Simply and discreetly, I'm optimistic about what I've done. I consider what is done outside to be so important and delicate that I endure the bitterness of this absence with resignation and turn my grief into energy, into a passionate desire to see myself fighting on Cuban soil as soon as possible. Once again, I promise that, if what we desire isn't possible and we are alone, you'll still see me come in a boat and land at some beach with a rifle in my hand.

That was the Fidel Castro whom Che met in Mexico in the summer of 1955. It's easy to imagine what someone, who viewed the democratic Latin American politicians — each one more demagogic than the last — with scepticism, who had known the

Bolivian revolution as it was turning back upon itself and who had witnessed and suffered with the crushing of the incipient Guatemalan nationalistic effort, felt when he met that young Cuban who, like himself, was living in the poverty of exile; who had already attempted to begin an armed insurrection in his country; who had been imprisoned; who spoke of his revolutionary project with faith, enthusiasm and as much confidence as if he had already carried it out victoriously; and who was preparing to renew the war of liberation in his homeland even though he didn't have any great economic resources and was struggling in incredibly disadvantageous conditions.

I arrived in Mexico City in the second week of August 1955. It was the first time I had ever left Cuba. I had carried out my instructions to set up a clandestine printing apparatus for the July 26 Revolutionary Movement in Cuba, and I went to Mexico to take up my new responsibilities as general treasurer of the Movement and aide to Fidel.

There, in the very small group of people who had our chief's confidence, I met Che. In a very short time, Che had already demonstrated exceptional political and personal qualities. You have to consider the rigorous security measures under which we did our work in exile to understand the deep impression Che must have made on Fidel for him to be incorporated so quickly in the circle of his most trusted comrades. And Fidel wasn't mistaken. Never would Che do anything to betray that trust.

A few days after I arrived there, on August 19, Che married Hilda Gadea, a Peruvian economist he had met in Guatemala. Che invited me to the wedding, and I was one of the witnesses, along with two Mexican doctors who worked with Che and Venezuelan poet Lucila Velasques, a friend of Hilda's. The ceremony was held in the municipal palace of Tepotzotlán, a small town near Mexico City.

When my wife, Melba Hernández, arrived, our relations with Che grew stronger — so much so that Che, Melba and I often went places together, including the library of the Mexican-Russian Cultural Exchange Institute in Mexico City.

Much has been said about Che's strong sense of humanity, character, willpower, courage, political ideas, determination to build a better society and lack of interest in material things, and I can add little to what has been repeated so many times over the years.

However, my memories of the time we spent together in Mexico lead me to say that none of Fidel's followers there made a greater effort than Che during our long hikes, exhausting sessions of mountain climbing, personal defense combat practice in the Bucarelli Street gymnasium, target practice and classes on the theory of guerrilla warfare in which the group engaged with great tenacity over a period of several months.

Moreover, though not a Cuban, he was unconditionally ready to come with us and fight for our freedom, thus contributing to our revolution's inspiring tradition of internationalism. Just as, after graduating, he gave up plans to go to Venezuela, where he could have found a very well-paying job, and went to Guatemala instead to participate in that revolutionary process which was cut short; and in Mexico, when he had finally emerged from months of economic insecurity and hunger and had obtained a job at the General Hospital and a post as a teacher of medicine, he renounced those rosy material and professional prospects and the tranquillity of family life with his wife and newborn daughter and dedicated himself to the cause of the Cuban people.

In June 1956, Fidel, Che and more than 20 others were arrested. Fidel had put him in charge of training the group of future expeditionaries at Las Rosas Ranch, in Chalco. Of all the group, Che was the last to be freed, and, when he was released, he couldn't go home. He had to remain in hiding, moving from house to house, until November 25, when he left for Cuba as one of the expeditionaries on board the *Granma*.

A letter he wrote to his parents on July 6 — the first of his documents in which he referred to Cuba and his commitment to the Cuban revolution — described that time in prison:

Some time ago — quite some time ago — a young Cuban leader invited me to join his movement, a movement which sought the armed liberation of his country. Of course, I accepted. Dedicated to physically preparing those young men who would go back to Cuba, I spent the last few months maintaining the myth of my professional post. On July 21 (when I hadn't been home for a month, because I was on a ranch outside the city), Fidel and a group of comrades were arrested. Our address was in his home, so we were all eventually caught in the roundup. I had documents accrediting me as a student of Russian at the Mexican-Russian-Cultural Exchange Institute, which was enough for me to be considered an important link in the organization, and news agencies that are friends of Dad's made a hullabaloo all over the world.

That was a synthesis of past events; future ones are divided into two groups: mid-term and immediate. In the mid-term future, I'll be linked to Cuba's liberation. I'll either triumph with it or die there.... I can't say much about the immediate future, because I don't know what will happen to me. I'm in the judge's hands, and I may easily be deported to Argentina if I don't get asylum in another country, which would be good for my political health.

Whatever happens, I must meet my new destiny, whether I remain in this prison or go free....

We're on the eve of declaring a hunger strike in protest against the unjustified arrests and the torture to which some of my comrades were subjected. The group's morale is high.

If for any reason (and I don't think this will happen) I can't write again and have the misfortune to lose, look on these lines as my farewell — not very grandiloquent, but sincere. I have gone through life searching for my truth by fits and starts and now, having found the way and with a daughter who will perpetuate me, I have come full circle. From now on, I wouldn't consider my death a frustration, but, like Himket, "I will take to my grave only the regret of an unfinished song."

Che wasn't deported to Argentina, nor did he have to seek asylum in another Latin American country. He set out with us on the *Granma* and, on December 2, 1956, arrived at Belic, an inhospitable, swampy area in Oriente Province. On the 5th, he was wounded in the first battle and, in the retreat that day — as he himself described it — in choosing the box of bullets instead of the knapsack of medicine, he also chose the destiny that would lead him to become known as the Heroic Guerrilla. He was the first fighter in the incipient Rebel Army who, in the Sierra Maestra, earned the [highest] rank of major and the command of a column, and his name appeared many times more in the records of Cuba's liberation in the next two years of the war.

Fidel trusted Che so much as a guerrilla leader and fighter that, at the most critical moment of the struggle in the Sierra — when the enemy launched its summer 1958 offensive against the Rebel Army's First Front — he gave him two extremely important missions involving great responsibility: that of organizing the first and only school of recruits in that front's territory and that of heading the defense of the western sector of rebel territory against one of the three main thrusts of the enemy advance. Carrying out both missions, Che once again proved worthy of that trust. After the enemy offensive had been defeated and the conditions had been created for taking the war to the rest of the country, Fidel named Che to lead one of the two guerrilla columns that were to undertake the difficult march toward the middle of the island of Cuba. Their successful campaign in the final months of 1958 made a decisive contribution to the military collapse of the tyranny and to the triumph of the revolution.

After the January 1, 1959, triumph, Che put all of his talent and energy into promoting the economic, political and social transformation of our country, holding a series of important posts in which he did a brilliant job. For six years, up to 1964, he made notable contributions in the spheres of theory and practice of our society's transition from underdeveloped, neocolonial capitalism to socialism, joining Fidel as a spokesperson of the impoverished peoples of the Third World.

He was only 39, at the height of his powers, at the time of his death in Bolivia in October 1967. It is impossible to imagine how much his loss has meant to the world revolutionary movement. He set us Cubans an example of the new human being without whom the society of the future, communism, would be impossible. Along with Julio Antonio Mella and Camilo Cienfuegos, he stands as a symbol for our young people, and his is the only name mentioned specifically in our Pioneers' [children's organization] pledge: "We will be like Che."

For all these reasons, we should make everything about him known. I think that *Che — A memoir by Fidel Castro* will be an important contribution to contemporary revolutionary writings, and that certainty was what led me to write this preface to this volume for English-speaking readers.

In 1987, the José Martí Foreign Languages Publishing House of Cuba and David Deutschmann of Australia joined forces to publish *Che Guevara and the Cuban Revolution*. Now, *Che — A memoir by Fidel Castro* has appeared as a companion piece.

I am confident that this new book will also become an important reference work for all who seek to understand Che's life and the fascinating Cuban political experience. It is a collection of excerpts from speeches, interviews and writings by our Commander in Chief that are related to Che. Nobody could have more authority than Fidel for evaluating Ernesto Guevara de la Serna in depth. We should recall that Che himself recognised that authority when he ratified his sense of identity with Fidel in his farewell letter of April 1965:

Recalling my past life, I believe I have worked with sufficient integrity and dedication to consolidate the revolutionary triumph. My only serious failing was not having had more confidence in you from the first moments in the Sierra Maestra, and not having understood quickly enough your qualities as a leader and a revolutionary.

I have lived magnificent days, and at your side I felt the pride of belonging to our people in the brilliant yet sad days of the Caribbean [missile] crisis. Seldom has a statesman been more brilliant than you in those days. I am also proud of having followed you without hesitation, of having identified with your way of thinking and of seeing and appraising dangers and principles.

Other nations of the world call for my modest efforts. I can do that which is denied you because of your responsibility at the head of Cuba, and the time has come for us to part.

The text of that letter, which was made public several months after it was written, completely refuted the infamous international campaign that the enemies of our revolution had launched claiming that Fidel and Che had quarrelled and that this was why Che had left Cuban public life. The countless disinformation campaigns and lies with which U.S. imperialism and its accomplices have sought to harm the Cuban Revolution throughout the past 30 years have always been cause for indignation, but this lie was one of the worst, for it tried to besmirch a unique, close friendship between two great figures in our history.

Because it reveals details of how that relationship between two exceptional men began and developed, *Che — A memoir by Fidel Castro* is also a definitive epitaph for that infamous lie. In addition, it is the most complete and consistent document defining Che, his strong sense of humanity and the reasons why he has become a symbol of revolutionary staunchness for all who struggle for a world of justice in which the honor of humanity will always prevail.

Jesús Montané Oropesa
Havana, May 1989

Introduction

by David Deutschmann

In the months following the overthrow of the Batista dictatorship on January 1, 1959, the new government led by Fidel Castro began to carry out a series of revolutionary measures. The dictatorship's repressive apparatus was dismantled. Racial discrimination was declared illegal. Rents and utility rates were lowered. An agrarian reform law confiscated all landholdings above 1,000 acres, providing land to hundreds of thousands of peasants.

As these popular measures were implemented, the new Cuban government faced growing opposition from Washington and U.S. corporations with holdings in Cuba. A growing polarization also developed within Cuba itself.

One of the earliest campaigns was centered on the threat of "communist infiltration" of the new government. The most prominent targets were Ernesto Che Guevara and Raúl Castro. Argentinian-born Guevara was singled out because he had not been born in Cuba, although a special government decree on February 9, 1959, had awarded him Cuban citizenship as a result of his outstanding contributions during the revolutionary war.

When Che Guevara was appointed to head the newly-created Department of Industry, which was attached to the National Institute of Agrarian Reform (INRA), a series of attacks appeared in the right-wing daily newspaper *El Diario de la Marina*. Fidel Castro took this up on September 28, 1959, as part of a television program called "Economic Commentaries":

We know from abundant experience who will stay through difficult times. We know from abundant experience who will fight to the death and who will jump ship. We know how far each person will go. And we have the right to know which

22

comrades can always be counted on to defend this revolution
— those of us you would first have to destroy, down to the
last person, before you could destroy the revolution. Listen
well! You would first have to kill us down to the last person.

Above all, it's good to know who the irresponsible
individuals are who have criminally dedicated themselves to
the task of diminishing the authority of the revolution in
order to lay the groundwork for struggles here inside the
country. Such struggles can have only an incredibly tragic
outcome for the nation. These individuals have clearly either
ignored or forgotten those who defend this revolution —
those who do so not out of personal interest or ambition but
for ideals they cherish, cherish genuinely, and cherish more
each day. That's why these individuals cannot lead the
country to anything but the worst of disasters, to the benefit
of our eternal enemies.

This divisionist campaign — that is, this campaign of
trying to sow divisions — who is it aimed at? Without doubt
the target is that fighter we Cubans have the most to thank,
that fighter who has performed the greatest deeds. Because if
there is one comrade who can genuinely be called a hero, it is
comrade Guevara.

And I don't say this because of the great things he has
done, which are well known to everyone. How in each
extremely difficult situation we never had to search for a
volunteer, because he would always step forward first. How
he showed extraordinary bravery. He was a comrade who
never pursued personal objectives. From the first to the last
day of the war, he was always ready to die, to sacrifice his
life for the cause — this comrade who always had to carry
medication for asthma, a vaporizer. And to think he led an
offensive through swamps. When we objectively assess the
feats that have been carried out, it is clear this is a comrade
whose stature will never be undercut by a dirty trick of this
sort — one directed not against him alone, but against all the
other comrades, against all those who are pillars of the
revolution.

It is a systematic campaign, not an isolated one. With
what aim? To lower the standing of those like comrade
Guevara who, when the country is under attack, are given
the task of defending an area or region and have to be killed

before it can be taken.

Comrade Guevara is someone who can be given any mission, any post, any assignment with the certainty that he won't hesitate a second. He is the kind of person this country needs, the kind we need in difficult times. And it is in difficult times that people show what they are made of. It is not always so in comfortable times, and certainly not by slinging slanders, infamy, and mud about comrades who deserve the respect of all Cubans because they have done only good for the country....

Just as the agrarian reform won the support and understanding of the people, we also wanted to promote popular support for industrialization. There can be no question that the process of agrarian reform was understood by the people. So we thought we should also set up a Department of Industrialization to talk with the peasants, to help lead them forward, to promote the idea of increasing savings to help buy goods needed for industrialization. And also to go to the unions and promote the idea of savings.

We sent Ernesto Guevara to the Department of Industrialization. Why? Simply because of his abilities. During the war — and since the days of the war this has been something I've been thinking about — the comrade who took charge of establishing the Rebel Army's initial industries was comrade Guevara. And out of this emerged, as you will recall, a series of industries, our primitive factories in the Sierra Maestra where we made implements of war, where we were able to manufacture land mines, shoes, a number of different things, in our small industry there.

And we said that if under those conditions, lacking nearly everything, without even a lathe to make parts — because obtaining a lathe required a tremendous effort; if we could do that under those conditions, we said, imagine what we could do in peacetime....

On November 26, 1959, Che Guevara was appointed president of Cuba's National Bank, replacing Felipe Pazos, an opponent of the course of the revolutionary government. Among the key challenges facing Guevara in this new position were stopping the flight of capital and the exodus of Cuba's hard currency reserves; stabilizing the purchasing power of the country's currency; and asserting control over the country's private banks, which had not yet been nationalized.

The appointment of Guevara intensified the propaganda campaign against him both in Cuba and internationally. An example was a July 1960 article in the *U.S. News and World Report* entitled "The 'Red Dictator' Back of Castro":

Look behind Fidel Castro and his brother Raúl for the real "Red dictator" of Cuba. Ernesto [Che] Guevara is the "brains" of Castro's Cuban government. Guevara is not Cuban, but Argentinian; not an emotional Latin by temperament, but a cool, calculating Communist.

To Guevara, Castro's Cuba is only a stepping stone to a Red conquest of all Latin America.

Guevara, not Fidel or Raúl Castro, is at the controls in this fast-moving period when vast U.S. investments are being seized. It is Guevara — described as an agent of international Communism — who must find the means to finance the economy of Cuba. Guevara, among other things, is president of the National Bank of Cuba. His hand is on every bank account, corporate and private, in the island. His are the decisions that determine the direction and the use of Cuban resources.

To Guevara, Cuba is only an incident in what he and his Communist aides regard as their real mission. This mission, according to those who work closely with Guevara, is to develop Cuba as a base for a Communist takeover of much of Latin America. What is taking place in Cuba is regarded as only a warm-up operation.

Fidel Castro dealt with this type of attack in the following excerpt from a speech on December 15, 1959 he gave to a meeting of the National Federation of Sugar Workers:

When it is time to make sacrifices, the first things to be sacrificed here will be luxury items. It is luxurious and nonessential goods that must be sacrificed. I know how the poorest peasants live, how sugar workers live, how the workers of this country live. They don't go around wearing French perfume. They don't go around wearing silk and lace. They don't smoke American cigarettes. And they don't spend money on luxury items. I know what poor families consume. We have statistics that show that. So when the time comes to cut back — well, that's why we have Che in the National Bank.

Who began to worry when Che was named president of the National Bank? It certainly wasn't the peasants, the sugar workers, or the poor. Those who were upset began to wage campaigns against Che. They began to slander him, to distort his ideas, to call into question the extraordinary merits he possesses, to make him into a bogeyman. But after making him a bogeyman, it turned out the people didn't see him that way. He was a bogeyman only to those who originated the campaign. When we named Che to the bank a great fear arose; they frightened themselves with the same bogeyman they themselves had created.

Some people went to the bank the other day to withdraw paper — paper! They went to take out "paper" because money is money only when there's an economy behind it, when there are monetary reserves, and those are the measures we are taking, defending those reserves. And to be sure, if there's no economy, if there are no reserves, the money is just so much paper.... If they withdraw paper from the bank, we'll print new paper. That doesn't mean anything....

If they begin counterrevolutionary maneuvers like taking money out of the bank, then we will simply issue orders to have new money printed up. And if that happens, not a single sugar worker is going to lose a centavo. For it is certain that not a single sugar worker has a bank account. No one is going to be fooled into thinking this fear affects the people. If those who are so upset had a little more common sense they'd be sleeping peacefully. We aren't going to touch those pieces of paper. On the contrary, to defend our economy, to defend our reserves, we are guaranteeing the value of those pieces of paper. Che was sent to the bank precisely to strengthen our effort to defend our economy and to defend our reserves....

Just so nobody makes any mistake about this, Che was not sent to the bank to play the fool. Just as in the past we sent him to Las Villas to prevent the enemy troops from reaching Oriente Province, we sent him to the National Bank to prevent our foreign exchange from escaping, and to make sure the reserves we have in foreign exchange are to be invested correctly.

Campaign of speculation and intrigue continues

On March 14, 1965, Che Guevara returned to Cuba following a three-month trip representing the Cuban government at the United Nations and in a number of African countries. Immediately upon his return he dropped from public view. In April he left Cuba to enter a new "field of battle," as he wrote.

Traveling in complete secrecy, Guevara's initial destination was the Congo, the African country today known as Zaire. The Congo had been the scene of a civil war after winning independence from Belgium in 1960. Its first prime minister, Patrice Lumumba, was arrested by U.S.-backed forces in December 1960 and subsequently murdered. When Moise Tshombe, who was directly involved in the murder, became head of state in 1964, this conflict developed into full-scale revolt by Lumumba's followers. Belgian troops and European mercenaries — with the aid of the United States — supported Tshombe's forces, slaughtering thousands of Congolese in the process.

Speaking to the General Assembly of the United Nations in December 1964, Guevara referred to "the painful case of the Congo, unique in the history of the modern world, which shows how, with absolute impunity, with the most insolent cynicism, the rights of the peoples can be flouted... All free men of the world must be prepared to avenge the crime of the Congo." With a hundred Cuban volunteer fighters, Guevara went to the Congo after he left Cuba in April 1965. There they assisted and helped train opponents of Tshombe's regime, staying several months into that year.

From the time Che dropped out of sight, speculation on his whereabouts began to appear in media around the world. In response to insistent questioning, Castro told a group of foreign journalists: "The only thing I can tell you about Commander Guevara is that he will always be where he is most useful to the revolution. Relations between the two of us are the very best; they're like the days we first met — even better. I believe his tour of Africa was very successful. He was also in China as part of our delegation. He is versatile, with an extraordinary understanding of things. He is one of the most complete leaders."

Nevertheless, rumors spread outside of Cuba — some of them deliberately provocative. The military dictatorship in the Dominican Republic claimed publicly that Guevara had been killed in the uprising that began there on April 24, 1965. Another rumor alleged that Guevara had defected to the United States and sold Cuban secrets for $10 million.

In response to this slander campaign, Fidel Castro made the following comments on June 16, 1965, marking the fourth anniversary of the founding of the Ministry of the Interior:

Now that I have mentioned Commander Ernesto Guevara, who so deserves that applause, you will have to listen to the confused rumblings of the imperialists. They say comrade Ernesto Guevara has not appeared in public, that he didn't show up on May Day, that he was nowhere to be seen the week cane cutting began. They are puzzled. Some say he is here, some there; or that there has been a fight, or perhaps problems. Yes, they really are puzzled.

We are going to reply to them: What business is it of yours? We are under no obligation to keep you informed or to give you any information. If you are puzzled, you can just keep on being puzzled. If you are concerned, you can just keep on being concerned. If you are nervous, take a tranquilizer or a sedative.

Our people, on the other hand, are not concerned. They know their revolution and they know their people. Comrade Guevara hasn't been seen at a public event? Well, then comrade Guevara must have some reason for not appearing at a public event. There is no news about him? He never was someone who sought publicity. Comrade Guevara has always been allergic — allergic! — to publicity. They say he is in poor health. That's what they would like to see. The imperialists would love to see him in poor health.

When there is concern over Commander Guevara it is a sign of respect and esteem for him.

When will the people know where Commander Guevara is? When Commander Guevara wants it known. Will you find out? Yes, you will find out. What do we know? Nothing! What do we think? We think Commander Guevara always has and always will carry out revolutionary tasks.

I don't understand this ignorance on the part of the

imperialists. Why don't they take a photograph with their U-2s. Why don't they go find him and photograph him? The fact is that it is much harder to photograph a man, no matter how big he is, than a missile.

Well, they can put their electronic brains to work on trying to solve this problem. We, for our part, will remain calm and content. Here no one is puzzled, no one. People don't even ask. Later they may ask. If so, an answer will be given. That's all there is to it.

After leaving the Congo in late 1965, Guevara went to Tanzania and then to Eastern Europe. In December 1965, he returned secretly to Cuba. Upon his return, Castro assisted him in beginning preparations for the guerrilla expedition to Bolivia. Guevara selected a group of Cuban volunteers who were veterans of Cuba's revolutionary war and of the recent mission in the Congo. A training camp was set up in a remote mountainous area of Pinar del Río Province in western Cuba.

In late October, Guevara — in disguise — left Cuba, traveling by way of Europe and arriving in Bolivia on November 4, 1966. He proceeded to set up a guerrilla base in southeastern Bolivia, near the border with Argentina, Chile, and Paraguay. Of the 50 guerrillas who eventually took part in the campaign, 17 were Cubans, including several members of the Communist Party's Central Committee. The first several months of the Bolivian campaign were devoted to organizing and consolidating the guerrilla unit. In March 1967 the first combat engagement occurred between the guerrillas and the Bolivian army. At the time, Guevara's presence in Bolivia was still not known publicly, and the speculation and rumors about his whereabouts continued. Reports abounded of his presence everywhere: some had him in Peru, Colombia, Guatemala — even as far away as Vietnam.

Before leaving Cuba for Bolivia, Guevara had written a message to the Organization of Solidarity with the Peoples of Asia, Africa, and Latin America (known as the Tricontinental), which had been formed following a January 1966 conference in Havana. The theme of Guevara's Message to the Tricontinental was the need for solidarity with the Vietnamese liberation struggle, under the watchword of "create two, three, many Vietnams." That theme was to figure prominently in the conference of the Organization of Latin American Solidarity

(OLAS) that took place in Havana in late July and early August 1967 and elected Guevara as its honorary chairman.

Guevara's message was released publicly on April 16, 1967. It was published in a special inaugural edition of *Tricontinental* magazine, which accompanied it with a series of photographs of Guevara in disguise before leaving Cuba. Its publication created a worldwide sensation and was reported prominently by the world's major news media.

On April 19, 1967, Fidel Castro commented on the publication of Guevara's article during a speech commemorating the sixth anniversary of the defeat of the U.S-backed invasion at the Bay of Pigs.

For the revolutionary movement around the world, for those who confront imperialism in Asia, in Africa, and in Latin America, the message of Commander Ernesto Guevara has been a dramatic event. We are not going to speak of ourselves, the Cubans. No one here ever believed the intrigues, ridiculous lies, and inventions of the imperialists. Here we all know one another, and we know the truth — because we've either heard it or guessed it.

The imperialists tried to sow confusion and lies throughout the world. They claimed to have located Che in a number of places, to have killed him at least a dozen times. For the imperialists, above all, this document must have been traumatic. Che's "resurrection," his presence, must have been deeply disheartening and upsetting. This Che with and without a beard, with a beard that might be new and might be old — you can't tell — and with that beret that seems to symbolize something, perhaps a sort of "Red Beret." This Che must have produced deep concern among the Yankee imperialists.

This Che in a magnificent state of health, with incomparable enthusiasm, and with more experience than ever in guerrilla armed struggle — this Che must be a source of concern for the imperialists, because he is a source of inspiration for revolutionaries.

Where is Che? the imperialists wonder. Organizing a liberation movement? Fighting in one of the liberation fronts? What the imperialists would give to know the answer to that! But even if they find out, it would do no more than simply satisfy their curiosity. Because if they really want to protect the health of their "Green Berets," they had better make sure the "Green Berets" never meet up with Che.

For those who sow intrigue and slanders, for those who try to benefit from and take advantage of Che's absence to hurl all kinds of slanders against the revolution — for them too it must have been quite a lesson, this presence of Che. And they — but why waste time on them? They've already been given their punishment. It's the punishment of history, because it's history that takes care of settling accounts with charlatans, slanderers, and those who take part in intrigues.

That's why the perversity of the slanderers is sad, but of no real concern. History will once again take care of these matters. That is the punishment of the intriguers and slanderers who have played the imperialists' game in every way possible in regard to this new stage, begun two years ago by comrade Ernesto Guevara.

Not everything is known, of course. But once again we leave it to history. We all received this document with immense happiness. None of us has the slightest doubt that time — whether it be days, weeks, months, or years — will inevitably bring fresh news of Che.

Chapter one

The rumor campaign surrounding Che Guevara's disappearance continued to grow during 1965. Spectacular stories began to circulate abroad, with the intention of creating divisions within the revolution. They alleged a political falling-out between Che Guevara and Fidel Castro, that Castro had placed a gag on Guevara, deported him, or even had him killed. These accusations were echoed in certain left-wing circles, often simply reported as fact.

At a mass rally on September 28, 1965, Castro announced that in a few days he would make public a letter Guevara had written him before leaving Cuba. "At that forthcoming occasion we will speak to the people about comrade Ernesto Guevara," Castro said. "The enemy has speculated a great deal and spread many rumors as to whether he's here or there, whether he's dead or alive. At times they are confused, at times they seek to confuse, and at other times they make insinuations. We are going to read a document from comrade Ernesto Guevara that explains his absence during these months. This will take place at the meeting I just referred to. [Shouts of 'Now!'] Now, no. Because I didn't bring the document here. I'm simply announcing it... I told you that at that time we would read this document and discuss some of the issues."

The meeting referred to by Castro was a televised ceremony to present the members of the Central Committee of the newly-formed Communist Party of Cuba. Guevara's name had been conspicuous in its absence from this list. This excerpt is from Castro's speech on October 3, 1965, to that meeting. Guevara's family was present in the audience.

ABSENT FROM OUR CENTRAL Committee is someone who possesses in the highest degree all the necessary merits and virtues to be on it but who, nevertheless, is not among those announced as members of our Central Committee.

The enemy has been able to conjure up a thousand conjectures. The enemy has tried to sow confusion, to spread discord and doubt, and we have waited patiently because it was necessary to wait.

This differentiates the revolutionary from the counter-revolutionary, the revolutionary from the imperialist. Revolutionaries know how to wait; we know how to be patient; we never despair. The reactionaries, the counterrevolutionaries, the imperialists, they live in perpetual despair, in perpetual anguish, in perpetual lying, in the most ridiculous and infantile way.

When you read the things said by some of those officials, some of those Yankee senators, you ask yourself: But how is it possible this gentlemen is not in a stable instead of belonging to what they call Congress? Some of them come out with absolute nonsense. And they have a tremendous habit of lying, they cannot live without lying. They live in fear.

If the revolutionary government says one thing, which is what it has consistently been saying, they see fierce, terrible things, a plan behind all this!

How ridiculous! What fear they live in! And you have to wonder: Do they believe this? Do they believe everything they say? Or do they need to believe everything they say? Or can't they live without believing everything they say? Or do they say everything they don't believe?

It's difficult to say. This would be a matter for doctors and psychologists. What do they have in their brain? What fear is it that makes them see everything as a maneuver, as a fierce, frightening, terrible plan? They don't know that there is no better tactic, no better strategy than to fight with clean hands, to fight with the truth. Because these are the only weapons that inspire confidence, that inspire faith, that inspire security, dignity, and morale. And these are the weapons we revolutionaries have been using to defeat and crush our enemies.

Lies. Who has ever heard a lie from the lips of a revolutionary? Lies are weapons that help no revolutionary, and no serious revolutionary ever needs to resort to a lie. Their weapon is reason, morality, truth, the ability to defend an idea, a proposal, a position.

In short, the moral spectacle of our adversaries is truly lamentable. Thus the soothsayers, the pundits, the specialists on the Cuba question have been working incessantly to unravel the mystery: Has Ernesto Guevara been purged? Is Ernesto Guevara sick? Does Ernesto Guevara have differences? And things of this sort.

Naturally the people have confidence, the people have faith. But the enemy uses these things, especially abroad, to slander us. Here, they say, is a frightening, terrible communist regime: people disappear without a trace, without a sign, without an explanation. And when the people began to notice his absence, we told them that we would inform them at the appropriate time, that there were reasons for waiting.

We live and work surrounded by the forces of imperialism. The world does not live under normal conditions. As long as the criminal bombs of the Yankee imperialists fall on the people of Vietnam, we cannot say we live under normal conditions. When more than 100,000 Yankee soldiers land there to try to crush the liberation movement; when the soldiers of imperialism land in a republic that has legal rights equal to those of any other republic in the world, to trample its sovereignty, as in the case of the Dominican Republic, the world doesn't live under normal conditions. When surrounding our country, the imperialists are training mercenaries and organizing terrorist attacks in the most shameless manner, as in the case of [the attack by counter-revolutionary Cuban exiles on the Spanish merchant ship] *Sierra Aránzazu*, when the imperialists threaten to intervene in any country in Latin America or in the world, we do not live under normal conditions.

When we fought in the underground against the Batista dictatorship, revolutionaries who did not live under normal conditions had to abide by the rules of the struggle. In the same way — even though a revolutionary government exists in our country — so far as the realities of the world are concerned we do not live under normal conditions, and we have to abide by the rules of that situation.

To explain this I am going to read a letter, handwritten and later typed, from comrade Ernesto Guevara, which is self-explanatory. I was wondering whether I needed to tell of our friendship and comradeship, how it began and under what conditions it began and developed, but that's not necessary. I'm going to confine myself to reading the letter.

It reads as follows: "Havana..." It has no date, because the letter was intended to be read at what we considered the most appropriate moment, but to be strictly precise it was delivered April 1 of this year — exactly six months and two days ago. It reads:

Havana
Year of Agriculture

Fidel:
At this moment I remember many things — when I met you in the house of [Cuban revolutionary] María Antonia, when you proposed I come along, all the tensions involved in the preparations. One day they came by and asked me who should be notified in case of death, and the real possibility of that fact struck us all. Later we knew it was true, that in a revolution one wins or dies (if it is a real one). Many comrades fell along the way to victory.

Today everything has a less dramatic tone, because we are more mature. But the event repeats itself. I feel that I have fulfilled the part of my duty that tied me to the Cuban revolution in its territory, and I say goodbye to you, to the comrades, to your people, who now are mine.

I formally resign my positions in the leadership of the party, my post as minister, my rank of commander, and my Cuban citizenship. Nothing legal binds me to Cuba. The only ties are of another nature — those that cannot be broken as can appointments to posts.

Recalling my past life, I believe I have worked with sufficient integrity and dedication to consolidate the revolutionary triumph. My only serious failing was not having had more confidence in you from the first moments in the Sierra Maestra, and not having understood quickly enough your qualities as a leader and a revolutionary.

I have lived magnificent days, and at your side I felt the pride of belonging to our people in the brilliant yet sad days of the Caribbean [missile] crisis. Seldom has a statesman been more brilliant than you in those days. I am also proud of having followed you without hesitation, of having identified with your way of thinking and of seeing and appraising dangers and principles.

Other nations of the world call for my modest efforts. I can do that which is denied you because of your responsibility at the head of Cuba, and the time has come for us to part.

I want it known that I do so with a mixture of joy and sorrow. I leave here the purest of my hopes as a builder and the dearest of my loved ones. And I leave a people who received me as a son. That wounds a part of my spirit. I carry to new battlefronts the faith that you taught me, the revolutionary spirit of my people, the feeling of fulfilling the most sacred of duties: to fight against imperialism wherever one may be. This comforts and more than heals the deepest wounds.

I state once more that I free Cuba from any responsibility, except that which stems from its example. If my final hour finds me under other skies, my last thought will be of this people and especially of you. I am thankful for your teaching, your example, and I will try to be faithful up to the final consequences of my acts.

I have always been identified with the foreign policy of our revolution, and I continue to be. Wherever I am, I will feel the responsibility of being a Cuban revolutionary, and I shall behave as such. I am not sorry that I leave nothing material to my wife and children. I am happy it is that way. I ask nothing for them, as the state will provide them with enough to live on and to have an education.

I have many things to say to you and to our people, but I feel they are unnecessary. Words cannot express what I would want them to, and I don't think it's worthwhile to keep scribbling pages.

Hasta la victoria siempre! [Ever onward to victory]
Patria o muerte! [Homeland or death]
I embrace you with all my revolutionary fervor.

Che

Those who speak of revolutionaries, those who consider revolutionaries as cold people, insensitive people, and unfeeling people will have in this letter the example of all the feeling, all the sensitivity, all the purity that can be held within a revolutionary soul.

And all of us could answer:

Comrade Guevara: It is not responsibility that concerns us! We are responsible to the revolution. We are responsible for helping the revolutionary movement to the best of our ability! And we assume the responsibility, the consequences, and the risks. For almost seven years it has always been like that, and we know that as long as imperialism exists, and as long as there are exploited and colonized peoples, we will continue running these risks and we will calmly continue assuming that responsibility.

It was our duty to comply with and respect the feelings of that comrade, to respect that freedom and that right. That is true freedom — not the freedom of those who seek to impose chains, but the freedom of those who leave to take up a rifle against the chains of slavery!

That is another freedom our revolution proclaims, Mr. [President] Johnson! And if those who wish to leave Cuba to go live with the imperialists, those whom the imperialists sometimes recruit to serve in Vietnam and the Congo, can do it, let everyone know that every citizen of this country, whenever they make a request to fight — not at the side of the imperialists but at the side of revolutionaries — this revolution will not deny them permission to go!

This is a free country, Mr. Johnson, really free for all!

And that was not the only letter. Besides this letter, and the occasion on which it was to be read, we have other letters greeting various comrades, as well as letters addressed "to my children," "to my parents," and to other comrades — letters he wrote for his children and his parents. We will deliver these letters to these comrades and these relatives, and we are going to ask them to donate them to the revolution, because we believe they are documents worthy of being part of history.

We believe this explains everything. This was what fell to us to explain. As for the rest, let our enemies worry about it. We have enough tasks, enough things to do in our country and with regard to the world, enough duties to fulfill. And we will fulfill them.

Chapter two

Following contradictory news reports on Che's death in Bolivia, Fidel Castro went on Cuban television on October 15, 1967, to deliver the following presentation.

AS YOU MUST HAVE figured out, the reason for this address is the news that has been arriving from Bolivia since October 9, and that has appeared for the last few days in our press.

I must begin by stating that we have become convinced that this news — that is, the news related to the death of Commander Ernesto Guevara — is, painfully, true. On previous occasions dispatches have been published asserting his death, but it was always easy to see that such reports were unfounded.

When wire-service reports about his death began to arrive on October 9, the character of the dispatches and the entire set of circumstances naturally made the news cause for concern. But still there was nothing definite. The news continued on the 10th, but the reports clearly contained a series of contradictions. They mentioned, for example, a scar on his left hand, but no one remembered a scar on Commander Ernesto Guevara's left hand. However, we recalled that he had scars on his neck and leg — bullet wounds from the war and, once, from an accidental shot that left a scar on his face. But none of these details were mentioned. Certain contradictions were noted and, above all, there was a general climate of disbelief in the news coming from Bolivia. So much so, that on the afternoon of October 10, any one of us would have expressed serious doubts about the accuracy of the reports.

Certain other indications began to appear, however, such as the first photographs. The first photograph, which arrived late on the night of October 10, did not bear a great resemblance — that is, many of us who first saw this photo tended to reject the idea it was Che.

We nevertheless expected that if it was an attempt to spread false news, or if it was a mistake, the features in the photo would be diametrically different. And we were concerned because there were some very general resemblances — that is, it might not be a photo of him, but we could not say categorically that it wasn't.

This photograph — this one [shows a photo] — I don't think it can be picked up very well by the TV cameras, and it's also not a very clear photo. However, a few hours later, another photograph arrived that depicted some unmistakable features of his face. This photo is also very dark, but with just a look at it you can make out... When a number of us saw this photo we began to think the news might be true, or, rather, for the first time we began to become convinced that the news might very well be true. This is the photo.

Then came a third photograph, in which the entire body is visible, on a stretcher. It too was a photo that could not be considered definitive; it's also a dark photo [shows photo].

The next day more photographs began to come in, until one arrived that was very clear, which is this one [shows photo]. It is so clear that possibly even when reproduced on newsprint it will still come across clearly.

I should explain that it is not simply a matter of our accepting the photograph as definite proof, but rather of the photograph as one of a whole series of circumstances that — in our opinion — confirm its authenticity, circumstances I will explain in a moment.

In the following days, newspapers continued to arrive from abroad, with more photographs. This one [shows photo]. Perhaps it is difficult to see this clearly on television, since it is taken from a newspaper, and naturally many of the details have already been lost.

Along with the photos, a great deal of other information began to arrive. Naturally, our approach was to collect all the facts in order to arrive at a conclusion that, in our opinion, would be absolutely certain — that is, an evaluation of the information with no room for doubt. That meant collecting all the evidence, all the photographs — those received here directly and those published in foreign newspapers — and all of the news was studied very carefully.

A few days later we received the first photographs of [Che's Bolivian] diary that was said to have been seized. Here are some of the photos of the diary [shows photos], these two photos, which are the ones that have appeared.

We did not want to give a definitive opinion until we had assembled all the available facts.

At the same time there was the question of Che's family. His father, his brother — I'm referring to his family in Argentina — who, according to the dispatches, were preparing to travel to Bolivia. We logically presumed that they would have the opportunity to make firsthand observations, and we understandably also waited for them to give their opinion first. So we waited. The trip was made, and a whole series of incidents occurred, many of which you are familiar with. They were not given the opportunity to see the body.

We nevertheless faced a delicate situation, with Che's Argentinian relatives finding, as they did, a number of strange circumstances — such as the news that the body had been buried, and then, immediately afterward, that it had been cremated. In such circumstances any relative would naturally tend to think the news was absolutely false. That is very natural and logical. For our part, we were already completely sure the news was true. But we did not want to state our opinion without first informing his relatives, through mutual friends who are in touch with them from time to time. And we were able to learn, moreover, that even now his father and other relatives believe the news to be absolutely false.

If it had simply been a personal matter, then unquestionably we would not have thought of insisting, nor would we have publicly stated an opinion contradictory to theirs. But the fact is that it is a question of great public importance throughout the world, and, in addition, a question that affects our people deeply. For that reason we felt it was our duty to state our opinion.

If we thought there was the slightest doubt, our duty would be to express that doubt. If we thought the news was false, our duty would be to say that it was false. And if, in our judgment, the news was true, there were various questions that had to be considered.

In the first place, as can be imagined, it was painful for us to have to state an opinion based on news coming from an oligarchic and reactionary government, a despotic government, an oppressor of its people, an ally of imperialism, and an enemy of the revolution. Nevertheless, we found ourselves in a position of having to support and confirm the truth of that news. I think that for any revolutionary such a thing is always painful.

There was also the consideration of whether there was any benefit in maintaining doubts about the news. Regardless of the circumstances, however — even if we felt it beneficial in any way to maintain doubts about it — such a consideration would not have kept us from telling the truth. As a matter of fact, we do not believe such a course of action would be in any way beneficial. I simply raise this hypothetically.

Even if keeping it in doubt could have been beneficial in any way, the revolution has never used lies, fear of the truth, complicity with lies of any kind as its weapons. We could not do so under any circumstances. Not only do revolutionaries abroad place their trust in our telling the truth, but so do our own people. They have always been sure that they have never been lied to, and that when a truth must be stated publicly, that truth always will be stated publicly.

And as people read the news, many were waiting for the revolutionary government and the party, their party, to tell them what was true and what were lies. Therefore, whatever the circumstances, we considered it our duty to express our opinion, although — as I said before — there was one thing that made this particularly delicate: that was the opinion held and stated publicly by the relatives of Commander Ernesto Guevara in Argentina. We hope they will understand that however painful it may be to have to make this statement, there is no lack of courtesy — much less lack of consideration — intended toward them.

I was telling you that we had reached this conclusion. We had not reached it on the basis of isolated facts, isolated words, or isolated photographs. A photograph can be doctored. But these were not photographs distributed by the government. These were photographs taken by a number of journalists right there in Bolivia, at the very spot where the body was. So there was no possibility of a doctored photograph; the thesis of a doctored photograph could not be accepted.

There were other hypotheses, for example a fabricated wax figure. This would be highly improbable, and it would not be easy.

This was all analyzed independently of all the other factors to be examined, and it turned out to be absolutely impossible. All this had to be analyzed in relation to a whole series of elements, of news reports that had been appearing, and all the other factors.

We found, for example, that this is Che's handwriting. It is undeniably his handwriting, which seems to us to be very difficult to imitate. But even if it were possible or easy to imitate someone's handwriting, above all of someone with a personality as distinctive as Che's, it would be absolutely impossible to imitate his style. And it would be even more impossible for anybody — except those who knew him extremely well, who had lived with him for many years — to be in a position to evaluate his every sentence, his style of writing, his way of expressing things, his reaction to each detail, to each thing. And, finally, a whole series of characteristics not only related to his handwriting but to the content, the style, the reactions. All that is absolutely impossible to imitate.

Naturally a diary does not prove the death of a combatant. A diary can be lost on a road, it can fall from a knapsack or can be left somewhere for safekeeping. This diary, however, was kept right up until October 7, the eve of the battle in which he was supposed to have been killed. That is, it contains things written up to just a few hours before the battle. It is unquestionable, therefore, that if the diary had been lost, it would have been lost approximately October 8, that is, the very day of the battle.

There is another series of elements to be considered. Different photographs of Che's presence in Bolivia had been coming in, published in various newspapers around the world. Some newspapers published this photo [shows photograph], which shows him with a bulky knapsack, the way he was accustomed to loading them, and with an M-2 rifle. Here is another photograph in which you can see him on a mule [shows photograph], and this is undeniably Che's erect stance. Probably at that moment he was joking about something with the person taking the photo. And, it would appear, some of these photographs were somehow seized by the enemy. In other words, there were all the indications, and it was generally accepted, that he was in Bolivia.

Another series of facts pointed to a strong pursuit of the guerrillas in recent weeks in Bolivia, involving a large number of troops. Among these troops were units specially trained by agents of imperialism in anti-guerrilla struggle.

These are some factors that should be analyzed a little to get an idea of things, of how Che's death came about.

That is, in our opinion the diary is absolutely authentic and

Photo: Roberto Salas

Photograph of future *Granma* expeditionaries after release from Mexican prison, June 1956. Che Guevara is seated (second from left) and Fidel Castro is standing (dark glasses, sixth from right)

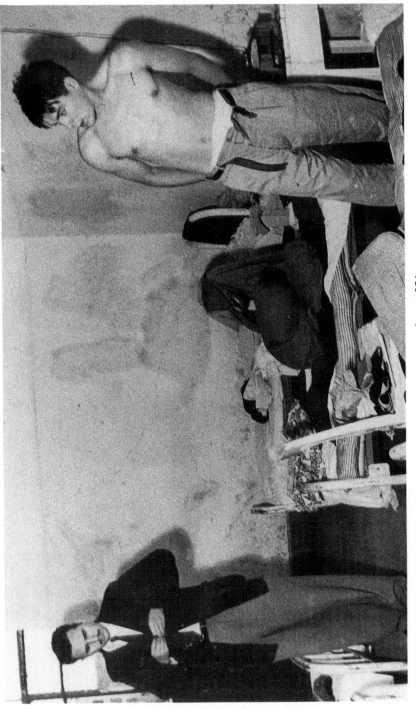

First photograph of Fidel Castro and Che Guevara together, Mexico, June 1956

Recovering from asthma attack in Sierra Maestra, 1957

Sierra Maestra, 1957: Che Guevara, Fidel Castro, Calixto García, Ramiro Valdés and Juan Almeida

Sierra Maestra, 1957

Che Guevara being sworn in as president of the National Bank of Cuba, November 26, 1959

Speaking, 1960

Juan Almeida and Che Guevara listening to speech

Che Guevara and Camilo Cienfuegos, 1959

1960

Voluntary work (Photo above: Liborio; photo below: Osvaldo Salas)

Break from voluntary work (Photo: Osvaldo Salas)

Fidel Castro, Raúl Castro and Che Guevara in 1963

Photo: Korda

Che Guevara and Fidel Castro, 1962 (Photo: Osvaldo Salas)

the photos are also absolutely authentic. It seems to us absolutely impossible in every way, technically impossible, impossible in reality, to fabricate all this. And, analyzing all the factors, all the details, all aspects — the diary, the photographs, the news dispatches, the way the news dispatches emerged, a whole series of facts — we concluded it was technically impossible to fabricate those proofs.

But let's probe a little deeper. There are so many contradictions within the Bolivian regime, so many rivalries, so many problems, that it would be absolutely impossible for those within this regime to reach agreement even to tell a lie. They can tell some lie, hand out some news release, report that something happened, that some guerrillas were killed where the bodies don't show up later. Reactionary governments are in the habit of giving out such news, and it has no great significance. That is one thing to consider.

Secondly, from the technical standpoint, they would need resources and experience that do not exist there.

Thirdly — and this is what is most obvious — why should that regime fabricate such news? What sense would it make to fabricate a report that would be exposed as a lie within 10, 15, or 20 days?

Besides, it seemed they were acting somewhat cautiously. Only 10 or 12 days beforehand they had issued a similar report, but they held to it for only a few hours. A few hours later, the next day, they quickly denied it. But this latest news report began to circulate very persistently, and they refrained from issuing a categorical statement. The first rumors came from various sources, from journalists. Apparently they were trying to obtain evidence that would enable them to issue an official statement without fear of a mistake. We noted all these things.

We already have some experience in interpreting news dispatches. We all read many dispatches every day, and we have some experience in evaluating the style and characteristics of every government, the personalities of those in the government. All those things, all those factors, helped us evaluate this news item. They seemed to be acting cautiously.

Not even the most imbecilic, the most idiotic of all governments — and there is no doubt the government of Bolivia is characterized by its imbecility and idiocy — would have resorted to such a senseless, stupid, impossible-to-invent thing as this, and then attempt to prove it. It would be completely senseless.

There is no doubt that the guerrilla movement in Bolivia is in a phase in which the survival of the guerrillas depends, fundamentally, on their own abilities; it depends on their own resources, let us say. That is, it is not a movement that has reached the point where a crisis is imminent, where a lie by the government would gain it eight or ten days, or a week. That was not the situation.

The guerrillas are in a period — a period we know only too well — in which they rely fundamentally on their own forces. And when guerrilla fighters hear such news reports, they laugh when they are false. Therefore, news reports have no effect on the guerrillas, while, on the contrary, they have an effect, an almost immediate effect, on the meager prestige and meager credibility some of these governments have.

I am reasoning this out in order for us to understand that it would be absolutely illogical for anyone to try to invent such news. I am doing this to consider what would be the motives to invent such news. There is no possible motive.

And the way the diary checks, the contents of the diary, the area spoken of in the diary, the photographs, photographs that were not issued by the government but which were taken by journalists — a whole series of specific features enables us to conclude with absolute certainty that the news is the bitter truth.

Logically, the natural tendency of any person faced with bad news about someone for whom he feels great affection is to reject it. To a great degree, that is what happened to us at first. In the mind of the people, in the mind of revolutionaries all over the world, there is a tendency to reject this kind of news.

In addition, that government's meager credibility, its absolute lack of prestige, helped cast doubt on the news, on top of the emotional circumstances that lead to an instinctive rejection of news of this sort.

This government is so discredited that even many of its allies — among them Yankee imperialism itself — many of the governments that are similar to the government of Bolivia, read the news initially and said they were not sure, that they did not believe it, and adopted a very cautious attitude. Later, naturally, they began to adopt a different attitude when they had in hand evidence that gave them some assurance of the news. But until they had that evidence, it may be said that almost universally they refrained from giving credence to the news coming from Bolivia.

But the discussion going on right now and the doubts that may remain — at least the doubts we have — are not connected with the fact of death itself but rather with the way he died, the circumstances that led up to it.

Those of us who know Ernesto Guevara very well — and I say know, because you really can't speak about Ernesto Guevara in the past tense — have had abundant experience with his character and temperament. However difficult it is to imagine a person of his stature, of his prestige, of his personality being killed in combat between a guerrilla patrol and an army force — however illogical that might seem — there is nothing extraordinary about it. For as long as we have known him, he has always been characterized by an extraordinary courage, by an absolute contempt for danger, and by a willingness, in every difficult and dangerous moment, to undertake the most difficult and dangerous tasks. That is what he did on many occasions during the course of our struggle. That is how he acted in the Sierra Maestra and in Las Villas.

Many times we had to take steps of one kind or another to protect him. On more than one occasion we had to oppose some action he wanted to undertake. And as we came to appreciate what a magnificent combatant he was, as we came to see the possibility that he might serve the revolution in tasks or missions of the greatest strategic importance, we tried above all to protect him from the risk of being killed in some battle of little strategic importance. That's more or less how the moment came in which he was made commander of one of the invading columns, charged with carrying out the exceptionally difficult task of invading Las Villas Province, a singular feat. Those who knew him then know the way he conducted himself in many actions.

And we must say that we were always worried about the possibility that this temperament, this ever-present attitude of his in moments of danger, could lead to his death in virtually any battle. No one could ever be sure he would adopt even minimal measures of caution. Many times he went out at the head of scouting patrols.

On the other hand, he was highly conscious of the importance of the mission he had taken on. And it is possible that he was thinking, as he always did, of the relative value of humans and the incomparable value of example. This was part of his personality.

We would have liked more than anything to have seen him become a creator — rather than a precursor — of great victories of the peoples. But a person of that type of temperament, personality, and character, of that way of consistently reacting to specific circumstances, is unfortunately more likely to be a precursor than a creator of such victories. Yet the precursors are also obviously creators of victories — the greatest creators of victories!

Che would be the one least upset by this. But for all of us who have come to hold a deep affection for him, it is understandably difficult to resign ourselves to seeing him become a precursor, an example whose impact we have no doubt will be very great. Any human being would understandably grieve when a character, a mind, and an integrity such as his is physically destroyed.

It is not my intention at the moment to express my ideas, opinions, and feelings about Ernesto Guevara. In today's broadcast I am explaining these things simply as part of analyzing the news dispatches we are receiving. But as I said, absolutely no one should be surprised that he would be one of the first to fall in a battle involving a guerrilla detachment. It would almost take a miracle, it would almost be impossible for it to have been otherwise. He confronted danger many times and on many occasions, and in these situations a sort of mathematical law operates. It wasn't something we thought would never happen, and we have been evaluating all the circumstances accordingly.

So, what is the background surrounding that moment, what are the circumstances that could have caused the battle that the enemy carried out in the midst of a large-scale mobilization, in the midst of a great deployment of forces against him?

Here, for example, we have some facts that perhaps can explain those circumstances that are part of that background. We cannot in any way make a categorical statement about these questions when the only information by which we can judge is what we have been able to collect, select, and analyze from the waves of news items, from a veritable sea of dispatches. But there is, for example, a dispatch here dated September 29:

A high ranking military source confirmed today that the

Bolivian army is firmly convinced it has the Argentinian-Cuban revolutionary Ernesto "Che" Guevara encircled in a jungle canyon some 128 kilometers from here.

The source declined to give further details. But his revelations to the Associated Press at noon today is supported by the fact that troops in battle gear have been dispatched in the last few days to the densely wooded area, apparently to engage in an important action.

Another 800 troops, especially equipped for jungle operations, left the city of Santa Cruz early this week for the same zone.

This city, where the trial of Régis Debray is being held, is headquarters for the Fourth Army Division, while Santa Cruz is the headquarters of the Eighth Division.

One contingent of troops left Camiri on Wednesday and another left last night. One more is scheduled to leave this afternoon.

According to a reliable military source, at least 1,500 troops are taking part in the man-hunt for Guevara.

"We have very good information that Guevara is alive, and we are more than convinced that he is surrounded," said the source, who refused to give details as to the basis for this belief.

According to this source, the army has surrounded the Communist guerrillas in a small valley between two hills of unspecified size.

This information could not be confirmed.

The two outlets of the valley, which is a sort of gorge, is occupied by Bolivian army troops specializing in jungle warfare. Many of them have been trained by U.S. instructors, some of whom served in Vietnam.

It was pointed out that the flanks and bottom of the valley are covered with dense growth, but the high parts are free of obstacles, impeding undetected flight.

"Army patrols exploring the jungle established positive contact at the beginning of this week," said the source.

That is, on the 29th they began to speak of a typical region, and of a wooded valley, a kind of gorge, between hills, or between elevations totally lacking in vegetation, where it was necessary to move in one direction or the other — that is, toward one exit or the other — without being able to leave the area because that would require moving over terrain absolutely lacking in vegetation.

This dispatch is especially interesting because it begins to speak of a territory, that appears in almost all the other dispatches. But what circumstances gave them the absolute assurance that they would find a guerrilla force directly commanded by Commander Ernesto Guevara in that territory?

Here is a news item that speaks of a deserter from the guerrillas. This news appeared on September 30, in another dispatch, which says:

> The Castro-Communist revolutionary leader Ernesto "Che" Guevara is gravely ill and is being carried on a stretcher by other guerrillas, under heavy guard, according to news dispatches released today in this oil center.
>
> This information is attributed to the Bolivian former guerrilla Antonio Rodríguez Flores, who voluntarily surrendered to the armed forces camped on the Río Grande, in response to the official offer to guarantee the lives of those who abandon armed subversion against the government.

A desertion took place some time between September 25 and September 30 — and a deserter always has the same attitude. A deserter offers the enemy all the information that can be of interest to the enemy, and offers it immediately, without scruples and without concern of any kind, because a deserter is above all a demoralized revolutionary, or a pseudorevolutionary who wanted to play at revolution. And it is indisputable that if a desertion occurs among the guerrillas — and during our revolutionary war there were many cases of desertion — this is nothing out of the ordinary.

There is a period in which many people want to join a guerrilla struggle and come to the guerrilla camps in great number; in fact, there are more who want to join than there are weapons for. Among those who come to join there are many who later play brilliant roles, who are magnificent soldiers, magnificent revolutionaries. Our guerrilla army never had a recruiting office or anything even similar. Our problem was the number of those who came to join us and for whom we did not have weapons. But more than 95 percent of the combatants in our Rebel Army came on their own accord; others were sent to us in an organized manner, only a few. Our army was made up of those who came and joined.

But, of course, some who were inspired to join had no prior experience and no clear idea of the sacrifices involved in the guerrilla struggle. And when they had to walk a lot, climb mountains, and face difficulties, they would take advantage of an opportunity to leave the detachment in a cowardly way. And a deserter is always a traitor. If he falls into the enemy's hands he immediately informs about everything, and he can give a full report on all the details involving the guerrilla detachment.

The dispatch speaks of illness. This must be taken to mean there may have been some temporary problem Che could have had.

In the part of the diary that has been published, in the photocopies of the diary, the entry for September 1 states: "We dismounted early from the mules after a few incidents, including a spectacular fall by one of them. The doctor has not yet recovered, but I have, and am walking perfectly, leading the mule." And he continues describing some other things.

That is, on September 1 he tells of how he has recovered and feels perfectly fine. And in the diary entries for the two days before his death, he talks like a person in perfect health. In other words, it was not true he was ill at the time.

But naturally a deserter could have described a previous illness, anything. Above all, the enemy was probably far more interested in pinpointing the exact location of the region or area where the guerrilla force was to be found. That explains why there was such a large mobilization of forces on September 29.

The news about the deserter was published September 30. It is possible that he had already been in the hands of the enemy forces for three or four days, and of course those forces immediately began to carry out a series of troop movements. Any repressive army mobilizes its forces when it sees an opportunity at hand; of course, most of the time such troop movements are an empty, useless effort. But it is unquestionable that they had high hopes, since they had the exact region where the guerrilla forces were located. They began to carry out a series of large-scale troop movements, with high hopes of winning a tactical victory there against the guerrillas.

Then there is the curious *New York Times* article written on

October 7 — that is, on the eve of the battle — and published in the edition of Sunday, October 8 — that is, on the morning of the day of the battle — headlined "Che Guevara's Last Stand?" It says:

> CAMIRI, Bolivia — Even for a man as traveled as Ernesto Che Guevara, the bleak cul de sac where the Andes fall off to the Amazon basin is a long way from anywhere.
> The sun rises blazing each morning on the dusty valley, baking the raw earth and the brown brambles. The teeming insect life — monstrous flies and mosquitoes, spiders and stinging beetles — swarm in the dead stillness....

The article goes on to give something of a description of the region. It says:

> The heat and the dust and the bites turn the skins of humans to a cloak of misery. The harsh vegetation, dry and covered with thorns, makes sustained movement all but impossible except along the well-watched river banks and trails.
> According to military reports, the erstwhile Cuban major and 16 exhausted guerrilla companions have been bottled up in the valley by a tightening armed forces encirclement for nearly two weeks. The Bolivian military believes Major Guevara will not get out alive.
> In many ways, the situation of Major Guevara... and his companions in their infernal canyon 120 miles northwest of the military post of Camiri serve as a metaphor for armed revolution in the hemisphere.

And so on and so forth. In other words, the content of the September 29 dispatch — which speaks of troop movements that were perfectly explained by the news of a desertion, published September 30 — is repeated by representatives of the foreign press who have close ties with the military command, and who speak insistently about the valley, the jungle-lined gorge, with areas lacking in cover.

That is, there is an air of hopeful anticipation — but this does not mean that the anticipated result will necessarily occur. Without having an idea of the terrain, without having an idea of the size of the valley, its width, its length, a whole series of circumstances, it is impossible to judge what real objective basis they could have had for harboring such hopes, since in general it is always said of guerrillas that they are surrounded.

For example, they always said they had us surrounded, which was true. We had the sea in back of us, the plains and rice fields in front of us, and for a considerable period of time our actions were conducted within a territory no more than 10 kilometers wide and some 20 kilometers long, with occasional incursions to places a little more distant. Throughout 1957 and until the middle of 1958, every offensive against us — including the last one, which involved an extremely large number of troops — took place in that 10-by-20-kilometer piece of territory. It was a territory that we knew very well, and at the time we had some 300 men.

But, generally speaking, the guerrilla unit is always seen as being surrounded; strategically, the guerrilla is surrounded by various military forces. More dangerous is tactical encirclement — that is, a guerrilla unit that is completely encircled by a cordon of enemy soldiers. But even in these situations, the cordons are broken through in a majority of cases. For that reason, no opinion can be given regarding the degree of danger involved in their location within the valley that is talked about, or in the region that is talked about.

But everything seems to indicate — because later they speak again of that region, and a certain persistence about this can be noted in all the wire-service dispatches — that they pinned their hopes on one particular region, and carried out a large-scale mobilization of forces. This does not necessarily mean that a clash had to take place, or that no withdrawal or maneuver was open to the guerrillas, but it explains the circumstances and the mobilization of forces preceding the battle.

This means that almost two full weeks before the battle, there was already a certain euphoria and a whole series of troop movements headed toward that region. What exactly is the region like? We do not know. What other regions or what natural obstacles mark it off? We do not know. Whether there were broad plains barren of vegetation, or a river, or insurmountable hills, we do not know. But what is clear is that troops were sent to a given region that, thanks to information from a deserter, had been more or less pinpointed as the location of the guerrilla forces.

Then come the dispatches, various dispatches, telling of a

battle taking place in a region they say is characterized by rugged terrain, by terrain where it is difficult to move, a dense jungle at the foot of a valley, deep ravines, gorges, canyons.

The diary entries of October 6 and 7 tell of such an area. For example, the entry for October 6 says: "Scouting patrols discovered a house nearby, but that also..." Some parts of the photocopy simply cannot be deciphered. Che's handwriting is small and not easy to read, and on top of that the photocopy has come out a little blurred.

The diary says: "...ravines farther away where there was water, we..." — something that we couldn't make out — "...and we cooked all..." — a line missing — "under a rock overhang that served as a roof... that I...."

It says: "In broad daylight we had passed close to places... were in a hollow." And again there are missing lines here.

It says: "Preparing the meal took a long time, so we decided to leave at dawn for a tributary near this little creek, and from there to explore when... to determine which direction to set out in."

It continues: "The Cruz del Sur radio reported in an interview... The men, this time Orlando was a little less..." — perhaps it says discreet. He is referring to another Bolivian who, it was first reported, gave himself up to the authorities. Later it was said that he was taken prisoner. There is something here that is not very clear, not as clear as in the other case.

It continues: "The Chilean radio carried a news item... to the effect that there are some 1,800 troops in the area."

The entry for October 7 says: "Today marks the completion of 11 months of guerrilla operations without complications." This "11 months of guerrilla operations without complications" indicates that the strategic situation of his forces, in his judgment, was not a difficult one. This is something to take into consideration — the fact that Che did not think it was a critical situation.

The diary says: "Up to 12:20, when an old woman, tending goats, entered the canyon where we were camped, and had to be taken prisoner. She gave us no reliable information about the soldiers, simply repeating that she knew nothing, that it had been quite a while since she had last been in the area. She gave us information only about the roads. From what the old woman told us, we are now about one league [about 3.5 miles] from Higuera, one from Jagüey, and some six leagues from Pusará. At 1:20..." —

here he gives a name — "Aniceto and... went to the old lady's house. One of her daughters is bedridden. They gave her 50 pesos and asked her to keep quiet, but they held out little hope she would do so despite her promises. The 17 of us set out under the waning moon. The march was very dangerous, and we left many traces in the canyon where we were. There were no houses, just a few potato patches irrigated by ditches leading from the stream. Between two paramos" — it seems to say; paramos seem to be those hills bare of vegetation — "...so we continued to advance in that direction."

Some things here cannot be well understood. The diary says: "The army has information to the effect that there are 250 revolutionaries." And here the page ends.

So he speaks of an area exactly like, or very similar to, that described earlier, which has to be crossed at night. And he gives the impression it is some kind of wooded valley bounded by rocky hillocks, bare of vegetation. That is the last thing he writes. It must have been almost dawn, because he says: "17 of us, under a waning moon. The march was very dangerous, and we left many traces...."

We have tried to decipher all this. Sometimes there are words that almost have to be guessed at in order to make out the meaning.

The diary refers to an area very similar to the one described in the wire-service dispatch of September 29 and in the *New York Times* article of October 8. Later there were many dispatches, and all of them always referred to a similar area.

On September 29, they talked about only one valley. Here they talk of several valleys, separated by hills, hills that are bare of vegetation, that are difficult to cross. They would either have had to make their way through the canyons or come out onto the higher ground, where it was impossible to move without being seen.

The guerrillas were apparently in a new area. This is made clear in the same entry, the same diary note of October 7, which indicates they had basically been exploring the terrain. Che is there with 16 other men, because he says "we left, 17 of us" and scouted the area. And he says, "we are now one league from here, two from here, six from there." They were trying to determine their exact location, they said, in order to determine what direction to set out in.

There is quite a consistency in how the earlier reports, the later reports, and the contents of the diary all more or less explain the circumstances in the same way: the existence of a deserter, accurate information on how many men were with him, and the place where he was located.

And there was the fact that they were in a new area. Any guerrilla unit scouting the terrain, any unit of troops in an area — even when it has information, detailed maps for example, even when it has aerial photographs, everything — can only really get to know a specific area on the ground. In fact, a guerrilla detachment scouting a wide area can wind up in an area like this one, an isolated area, a relatively isolated area, through going scouting. It may advance through mountains and suddenly reach a point where even the areas of vegetation, or the area of territory suited for guerrilla warfare, disappear, and it then becomes necessary to return to another area and continue scouting. This is one of the things we did in the Sierra Maestra in the beginning. We would send out scouting patrols to get to know a certain territory, until we were finally perfectly acquainted with it.

We don't know whether the territory was really isolated, whether the territory where they were at the time could be cut off. We don't know whether it was made up of a valley or a series of valleys that could be entered or left here or there and was surrounded by areas that could not be crossed, by large stretches that could not be crossed in a night's journey. To know if the enemy's hopes were well-founded, we would have to have information about the territory. But many times repressive armies entertain hopes of this type, and most of the time they are not well-founded. So we can say that even though a battle did take place, this was not necessarily the only possible outcome.

Clearly there were large-scale troop movements, and these troops moved in a direction determined by information they had. The territory they were in raised the hopes of the repressive forces because of an accidental encounter between the guerrilla forces and the repressive forces. If an accidental encounter took place, then the possibilities that Che might be killed increased, because of those traits of his that I explained earlier.

It is clear that neither the guerrilla forces nor the repressive forces fell into an ambush. It is clear that a clash took place. And according to all indications it is clear that when this clash took place, Che carried out some sort of action. All the indications, all that is said, points to some action such as moving forward to see, or moving forward to fire, or even moving away from the place — perhaps a few steps, a few meters — from where the rest of the combatants were. That is, everything seems to indicate that he carried out one of his characteristic actions, and it appears that he was seriously wounded very early and remained in a kind of "no man's land." It is also clear that his comrades, probably seeing him wounded, seeing he was in danger, and inflamed by that fact, fought a prolonged battle that went far beyond any battle that a guerrilla detachment would fight under normal conditions. That battle lasted four hours, according to some, and five or six hours according to others.

A guerrilla unit generally does not fight a battle of this type, since the enemy is always superior in numbers. If the enemy is given time, it may be able to surround the guerrillas. Only a guerrilla detachment inflamed under circumstances such as these would fight a battle of four, five, or six hours. Among other reasons, the ammunition of a guerrilla detachment tends to run out in a battle of that length. This is another factor that we evaluated and took into consideration.

When you read a news dispatch, anyone who has guerrilla experience knows what happened. You know what happens when a repressive force falls into an ambush. This is unmistakable. Generally the repressive force that falls into an ambush loses its advance guard and loses many men. It may or may not also lose weapons; that depends on the number of guerrillas and on other circumstances.

In the same way, when a guerrilla force falls into an ambush by repressive forces, since the guerrilla force is always numerically smaller, in general it cannot inflict casualties on the ambushers. This is simply a law of warfare.

If that's the case, if in this instance there was no ambush on either side, if it was a clear-cut matter and really a prolonged battle, it is evident that something unusual happened.

And the fact that the military reports spoke of so many soldiers wounded and killed, of 10 casualties, while also stating the number of casualties of the guerrillas — first said to be five — was rather strange and something to be concerned about. In the initial reports it was stated that Che was among the first to be wounded and that he was in a "no man's land." These are the only circumstances that would make a guerrilla unit carry out a prolonged battle, one lasting from one in the afternoon until nightfall — the only circumstances! And this aspect was something to be concerned about. Because, in general, one or the other group falls into an ambush, and the characteristics of the situation are quite clear. But a guerrilla unit never wages a battle for five or six hours against troops that are numerically superior, have more ammunition, and in fact enjoy a whole series of advantages, including the ability to surround the guerrillas.

Anyone with experience in guerrilla warfare knows that this battle was not an ambush by one side or the other, that it was not the type of battle characteristic of guerrilla warfare. And it is obvious that the abnormal circumstance in this case was the fact that Che was wounded. His comrades made a superhuman, desperate effort, risking everything. They kept fighting, inflicting 10 casualties on the enemy — according to the enemy's own account — and perhaps even more.

This is part of what I referred to before as the set of facts, circumstances, and other things that helped us form a judgment about the situation.

The question that is being debated — as I said at the beginning — is what happened afterwards. The question is whether Che died instantly or was seriously wounded and, after some hours, taken alive by the repressive forces. This is the question most under debate.

Naturally, all of us who know Che understand that there was no way possible of capturing him alive unless he was unconscious, unless he was totally paralyzed by his wounds, unless his weapon had been destroyed and therefore had no way to avoid falling prisoner by killing himself. No one who knows him well has the slightest doubts about that.

There is something more. The enemy itself, the officers of the enemy force themselves — all are unanimous in attesting to Che's extraordinary courage, his conduct and his scorn for danger. There has not been a single word that would attempt to deny him these characteristics. It is therefore difficult to believe that they could have captured him — although it would not have been impossible, especially in the situation he was in, wounded in "no man's land," unable to move, possibly unconscious. It is by no means impossible for them to have captured him while he was still alive.

And it is on this point that a whole series of tremendous

confusions and contradictions have arisen, which perhaps explain the attitudes displayed and the events that happened afterward. Naturally, I did not bring all the dispatches with me, because they make quite a bundle. But from the very beginning, when there was not a single official report, the rumors started — rumors picked up by the reporters — that Che was either dead or wounded, or that he had been captured after being wounded. The very first reports received spoke mainly of him as a wounded prisoner.

Later, official statements began to be made. On October 10, for example, a wire-service dispatch reported:

> High-ranking officers of the Bolivian army declared that it had been fully confirmed that the Argentinian-Cuban guerrilla leader met his death in Bolivia yesterday after being seriously wounded the day before.
>
> General Alfredo Ovando, chief of the armed forces, reported that Che had identified himself and had admitted failure with the Bolivian guerrillas, who General Ovando said had been virtually wiped out.

Nobody believed the part about Che having said such a thing. Even though we are thoroughly aware of his extraordinary frankness and invariable honesty, we must say that if he were able to speak under such circumstances, he would never say anything pleasing to the enemy. In fact, whatever the circumstances he would calmly say whatever would displease the enemy the most.

But the problem is that this gentleman stated that Che died the following day as a result of his wounds. That is what he said. High officials confirmed the same version of events. Then the chief of the army division operating in the area comes on the scene and says that "the battle took place in a canyon called El Yuro, where the soldiers fought bravely, almost hand-to-hand, at a distance of no more than 50 meters."

Zenteno added that "Guevara was found alive but seriously wounded, in a deep pass."

"Asked if Guevara said anything to his captors, Zenteno contradicted Ovando's statement by responding that Guevara never had time to say anything."

Ovando says Che was captured alive, seriously wounded.

Another official says the same thing. But Ovando says Che told him who he was and that he had failed. The other official says Che said nothing, not even a word.

Of course, a few days later this same gentleman declared — once his contradiction with his chief had become evident, it seems — that yes, Che was alive and had said the same things Ovando claims he said. But both of them declare that Che was alive.

Naturally, it seem senseless to claim Che said such a thing, because nothing else they say is even remotely detrimental to him. They themselves acknowledge his integrity, his courage, everything about him.

Che might just as easily have said: "My name is this, that, or the other." That would have been in keeping with his character. What could he have said, and what did that gentleman hear?

But both of them agree Che was alive. And these statements take on further importance when we take into consideration a whole series of later events. This is when the version emerges that he was captured when he was seriously wounded but still alive, and that he was then finished off — that is, he was shot to death. In other words, not the slightest effort was made to take care of his wounds, no effort whatsoever was made to save his life. There is not the slightest evidence that he received any treatment, but there are a series of indications that what they actually did was to kill him. And this in spite of the fact that earlier reports always mentioned how Bolivian soldiers wounded in combat had been taken care of by the revolutionaries and then released. Of course, what else can you expect from a mercenary army, from mercenary officers, from a mercenary government?

No one can give assurance that Che would have been able to survive his wounds, because the wounds must have been very serious. No one can say that he would have survived. But what is undeniable is that they made not the slightest effort to save him. It seems what they did was to kill him.

How did all these contradictions come about? A whole series of things have now become clear, because the doctors, as well as soldiers wounded in the battle, have begun to make statements. Here, for example, is a wire-service dispatch we received yesterday. It says:

Dr. Martínez Caso, one of the two physicians to see the body upon its arrival in Valle Grande, was interviewed there. He was asked if an autopsy had been performed. "No, we made only a simple examination. Death must have occurred about five hours earlier, because the body was still warm," the physician answered.

This means that if the body arrived at the hospital in Valle Grande around 5 p.m., October 9, death must have occurred around noon the same day.

The physician added that the body showed bullet wounds, five of them in the legs, one in the throat, and the other one in the chest, below the left breast. This bullet pierced the heart and lung. "This is the fatal wound," the doctor added.

When the body was turned over to him he was told it was probably the body of an important person. This opinion was based on the perfect condition of the feet, which left the impression that the man was not accustomed to walking too much.

So the body was delivered to the doctor and he discovered that death had occurred only a few hours earlier, that there was no sign of rigor mortis. And the fact remains that Ovando, the high-ranking officers, Colonel Zenteno, everybody says that when they captured him, he was still alive. And the doctors say — and everybody who knows a little bit about medicine agrees — that nobody can live more than a few minutes with their heart pierced by a bullet. This is when all the suspicions began to emerge.

Here is a dispatch from Interpress that reads:

LA PAZ — A spectacular change seems to have come over the investigations made by observers into the circumstances surrounding the death of Ernesto Che Guevara in a battle last Sunday, since José Martínez, a Bolivian physician who examined the body of the Argentinian revolutionary Monday afternoon, stated that death had occurred only five hours before.

This confirmation strengthens the opinions insistently expressed by well-known journalists present in the army's anti-guerrilla center of operations that Guevara was given a 'coup de grace' after he was captured alive, together with two other guerrillas. Several official spokesmen share the same doubts as to how the principal organizer of the insurrectional movement died.

To this may be added a new version, issued recently by a high, confidential military source, which says that Guevara's death was not caused by the wounds received in battle against the army in the El Yuro ravine. The guerrilla leader died at 1:15 p.m. in Higueras, where he had been taken before the battle had ended.

According to the same military source, Che had been wounded in the legs.

This is followed by a sentence whose meaning we can only guess at because it is mutilated. It says: "But when a bullet put his rifle out of commission...."

That is, it seems this dispatch suggests that after being wounded, Che kept on fighting, firing his rifle until it was put out of commission. That is possible. There is nothing extraordinary about him fighting against the enemy while wounded. And many combatants have had their rifle destroyed in battle.

The dispatch continues:

But when a bullet destroyed his M-12 rifle that had been adapted for use as a submachine gun, he was taken prisoner along with two other guerrillas who were apparently also wounded. When interrogated on Monday, Guevara did not answer a single question.

If something like this happened, those of us who know Che well are aware that this is the only attitude he would adopt.

And it says: "...he did not answer a single question, looking indifferently at his captors." It continues: "The other two guerrillas were also killed that same day at Higueras."

That is, this news agency gives the version of how he was wounded, how he continued fighting while wounded. That is what it leads one to believe.

Here is another dispatch: "Dr. José Martínez Caso stated during an interview that the fatal shots were one lodged in the heart and another in the lungs, but that when he examined the body..." That is, the same news. Then this news agency says: "Martínez's statement coincides with those of four wounded soldiers...."

Ah. Here it says that, according to the doctor, the soldiers told him that when Guevara saw them he advanced toward them and was hit.

It continues: "Martínez's statement coincides with those of four wounded soldiers who took part in the battle. The four said that they saw Guevara alive after the battle." One of them, named Taboada, said he was near Che when Che was hit, saying explicitly that "Guevara was wounded in battle and that he was still alive then."

So there have been a series of statements that repeatedly coincide with the first version, which tells of Che being taken prisoner after being seriously wounded.

For him to be wounded while advancing on the soldiers would be something natural for him. And for him to continue fighting despite being wounded would be characteristic for him. While he still had a breath of life, he could be captured only if he were unconscious, or if his weapon were destroyed, or if he couldn't move because of a serious wound. For them to question him and for him to look back at them with absolute indifference — more than indifference, complete scorn for his captors — all that is consistent with his personality, as would be his having died in battle.

The most important thing is not whether he died in battle or was finished off later, after having been seriously wounded in battle. In itself, that is not the most important thing. What is important is the certainty that he had received fatal, or nearly fatal wounds that undoubtedly led, in one way or another, to his death.

But a serious controversy has arisen around this point, and this explains in part, but only in part, what was later done with his body.

Then comes a series of dispatches.

One on October 11 says: "The President of the Republic, General René Barrientos, told United Press International tonight that the remains of Ernesto Che Guevara, buried last night in a secret spot in the Bolivian Andes, will not be brought to La Paz, nor be exhibited again.

"One of the stupid things that I said," added the head of state, "is that the body would remain in Bolivia."

It seems — according to a dispatch from Bolivia — that Che, in one of the entries in his diary, said that Barrientos is stupid. So that gentleman, alluding to that part of the diary, says that one of the stupid things he said was the matter referred to above.

So on October 11 the claim is made that the body was buried in a secret place. The next day, October 12, a dispatch stated the following:

> Journalists who say they have interviewed Roberto Guevara, Ernesto's brother, reported him to have said that Gen. Alfredo Ovando, commander in chief of the armed forces, told him that the body of the Cuban-Argentinian revolutionary had been cremated today.
>
> That version was challenged tonight by official government sources.
>
> "President René Barrientos knew absolutely nothing of this until at least 5 p.m. today," stated a high official in the Foreign Ministry.
>
> "We would be greatly surprised if that were true," added the source, "because it would have to have been a last-minute decision made by the Armed Forces, without notifying the president himself, which is difficult to believe."

Then all the dispatches began to arrive indicating that Che had been buried, that the body had been exhumed, that it had been cremated, that they had cut off one of his hands, or a finger — a whole series of dispatches, both macabre and contradictory.

One can easily imagine that they would want to conceal proof that Che was killed while in custody. They were worried that a careful examination of all the details would reveal that a coup de grace had been administered.

But in my opinion there is something they give even more weight to, which is what is behind all these strange things. And that something is their fear of Che even after his death. Not only were they afraid of him while he was alive, but even after his death they are still afraid, even more afraid. This is an idea they themselves began to give prominence to when they removed Che's remains so the area could not become a shrine.

They know instinctively that they are condemned by history. And they know it was a mere stroke of luck that they could physically eliminate Che. So it is logical that they would be afraid that Che's remains, or the site where they are buried, would become a shrine now or at some time in the future. They wish to deprive the revolutionary movement of even a symbol, a site, a spot. In a nutshell, they fear Che even after his death.

In my opinion, the key factor in their behavior is not their concern to conceal whether or not they fired the final shot. The key factor is really their desire to get rid of Che's remains. They are afraid that his family might claim the body, that it might be buried at a specific site and become — as they might call it — a shrine, a revered spot for revolutionaries. That, in my opinion, is the real reason behind all those things.

These are more or less our impressions of how events occurred, our evaluation of the news items, of the whole series of strange and contradictory events after Che's death.

We considered it our duty to speak of this information, to express this conviction, regardless of whether a state of uncertainty might be useful to the revolutionary movement. We considered it a moral question, a question of principle, a duty to the people, a duty to revolutionaries everywhere. In our opinion, the only one to benefit from indefinitely maintaining uncertainty and doubt, from maintaining false hopes among the masses, would be imperialism.

We are not about to believe that the imperialist puppets in Bolivia, who are vying to be seen as the vanguard lackeys of imperialism, want us to doubt their news. It is clear that the imperialist puppets in Bolivia want the news to be believed, because it has to do with their role, their part, their aspiration to be vanguard puppets.

But as for the imperialists, who are quite subtle, there should not be the slightest doubt that, after eliminating Che physically, they would like to diminish the impact of his conduct, his example, his consistent, heroic, and revolutionary attitude. They would like to weaken that example, that impact, by clouding it with mystery, with uncertainty, with illusory hope. They would like 5 years, 10 years, 15 or even 20 years to pass with his example clouded by mystery, hovering between doubt and hope. Such hope is natural and understandable among all who find Che's death particularly painful. It is understandable among all who sympathize with and admire him, among revolutionaries throughout the world.

Imperialism knows it has freed itself physically of Che. Its great aspiration now is to free itself of his spirit, to find some subtle way of dissolving it into a vain and illusory hope — a hope that, while never fulfilled, could, on the other hand, feed speculation and stories reporting, "We saw him here" and "We saw him there."

When a fabricated story relates things that can later be disproved, we are not worried. For a long time there were all sorts of suppositions and stories going around, all kinds of versions and interpretations of Che's absence, a host of gross statements, indecent slanders. We were never seriously concerned about this. We knew the facts, the truth, would eventually come out, and all the mistaken theories and interpretations, whether put forward in good or bad faith, would be shattered. We were not concerned.

But we did have to concern ourselves about the possibility that a false hope might arise, with nothing concrete to contradict it. And that such a false hope — with the passage of years and surrounded by the deepest mystery — would only weaken the impact of one of the most extraordinary examples known to history of loyalty to revolutionary principles, of integrity, courage, generosity, and selflessness.

The facts will soon give lie to the imperialists' triumphant boasts that Che's death will discourage the revolutionary struggle. The imperialists, too, know the power, the tremendous power, of example. They know that while a person can be physically eliminated, an example such as Che's can never be eliminated by anything or anyone! They are understandably deeply concerned about this.

Newspapers of all tendencies and currents have universally recognized Che's virtues. Only in an exceptional case, among hundreds of viewpoints expressed, does the vulgar opinion of some scoundrel crop up. For Che's life had the virtue of impressing even his worst ideological enemies, causing them to admire him. It is an almost unique example of how a person can gain the recognition and respect of their enemies, of the very enemies they have faced, arms in hand; of their ideological enemies, who have in turn been almost unanimous in expressing feelings of admiration and respect for Che. It is understandable that this should worry imperialism.

Many people, including a number of political figures, have stated that Europe has been astounded at the impact of the news about Che, at the tremendous interest in it. It has been a kind of awakening to the realities of our times.

We sincerely believe and hold the opinion that the duty of telling the truth stands above all considerations of convenience — and that has been our attitude. We must tell revolutionaries our conviction, our absolute certainty, our evaluation of the news reports. Furthermore, we must issue this warning so that imperialism will not be able to make use of doubts to bring about inaction and uncertainty.

It is even possible that the fact that many revolutionaries were not convinced, or had doubts about the news, that may have kept them from speaking out. For no revolutionary — so long as there is hope of any kind — accepts news of this sort. And we know that revolutionaries have faith in the Cuban revolution, that revolutionaries throughout the world have genuine faith in the word of the Cuban revolution. We have come here once more to make good that faith, to demonstrate the justice in that faith in the absolute honesty of the revolution. No matter how bitter, how painful the circumstances — including those we mentioned, of doubts among close relatives — we cannot waver in fulfilling this duty.

Moreover, what good would it do for revolutionaries to maintain false hopes? What would be gained by that? Aren't revolutionaries the ones who must be prepared for whatever comes about, for all vicissitudes, including setbacks? Has the history of revolutions and revolutionary peoples been characterized by the absence of hard blows? Aren't true revolutionaries the ones who overcome these blows, these setbacks, without becoming discouraged? Isn't it precisely revolutionaries who preach the value of moral principles, the value of example? Aren't revolutionaries the ones who believe in the lasting quality of the work of human beings, of the principles of human beings? Aren't revolutionaries the first ones to acknowledge how ephemeral is humanity's physical existence, and how long-lasting and durable are humanity's ideas, conduct, and example — since example is what has inspired and guided the peoples throughout history?

This is always the way it has been. Harder blows, extremely hard blows were dealt to our revolution for independence with the death of Martí and with the death of Maceo. Such blows have been dealt to many revolutionary movements, and they always overcame these setbacks and blows, no matter how hard they were.

Who could deny what a blow Che's death is to the revolutionary movement, how much it means to no longer be able to count on his experience, his inspiration, the strength of his reputation, which instilled fear into reactionaries? It is a fierce blow, a very hard one. But we are sure that he more than anyone was convinced that what is most important is not man's physical life but rather his conduct. This is the only way to explain and understand how Che's absolute contempt for danger fits in with his personality and actions.

We must not lose time or allow the enemies of our ideology, the enemies of the revolution, to take the ideological offensive or to assume the psychological offensive in order to dishearten the revolutionary movement. Basing ourselves on the truth and recognition of the truth, and turning Che's example into invincible strength, the revolutionary movement must go forward, firmer and more determined than ever.

I have carried out this bitter task. Perhaps it has not been an absolutely exhaustive analysis, but suffice it to say that analyzing everything, absolutely everything, we — all the leaders of the revolution, all of us who are intimately familiar with Che's character — we have all, unanimously, and without the slightest doubt, come to this same conclusion I have expressed to you.

Today, the Council of Ministers met and adopted the following resolution:

"Whereas: The heroic Commander Ernesto Guevara died fighting for the liberation of the peoples of Latin America at the head of the Liberation Army of Bolivia;

"Whereas: The people of Cuba will always remember the extraordinary service rendered by Commander Ernesto Guevara, both in our war of liberation and in the consolidation and advancement of our revolution;

"Whereas: His conduct embodies the spirit of internationalism that inspires the united struggle of the peoples;

"Whereas: His untiring revolutionary activity, which knew no borders, his communist thinking, and his unshakable determination to fight until victory or death in defense of the national and social liberation of the people of Latin America and against imperialism, constitute an example of revolutionary conviction and heroism that will last forever;

"Therefore be it resolved:

"First, that for 30 days, beginning with the signing of this resolution, the national flag be flown at half mast; and that for three days, starting at 12:00 midnight tonight, absolutely all public entertainment be suspended.

"Second, that the day of Che's heroic death in combat be declared a national memorial day, to that effect establishing October 8 as the Day of the Heroic Guerrilla.

"Third, that as many activities be carried out as may be conducive to perpetuating Che's life and his example in the memory of future generations."

At the same time, the Central Committee of our party has resolved:

"First, to create a commission made up of Commanders Juan Almeida, Ramiro Valdés, Rogelio Acevedo, and Alfonso Zayas, headed by the first of the aforementioned comrades, to orient and direct all activities aimed at perpetuating the memory of Commander Ernesto Guevara;

"Second, to issue a call to the people to hold a solemn memorial gathering at the Revolution Plaza on Wednesday, October 18, at 8:00 p.m., to pay tribute to the unforgettable and heroic fighter who has died in combat."

Chapter three

At a memorial rally for Che Guevara in Havana's Revolution Plaza on October 18, 1967, attended by almost one million people, Fidel Castro made the following remarks.

I FIRST MET CHE one day in July or August 1955. And in one night — as he recalls in his account — he became one of the future *Granma* expeditionaries, although at that time the expedition possessed neither ship, nor arms, nor troops. That was how, together with Raúl, Che became one of the first two on the *Granma* list.

Twelve years have passed since then; they have been 12 years filled with struggle and historical significance. During this time death has cut down many brave and invaluable lives. But at the same time, throughout those years of our revolution, extraordinary persons have arisen, forged from among the people of the revolution, and between them, bonds of affection and friendship have emerged that surpass all possible description.

Tonight we are meeting to try to express, in some degree, our feelings toward one who was among the closest, among the most admired, among the most beloved, and, without a doubt, the most extraordinary of our revolutionary comrades. We are here to express our feelings for him and for the heroes who have fought with him and fallen with him, his internationalist army that has been writing a glorious and indelible page of history.

Che was one of those people who was liked immediately, for his simplicity, his character, his naturalness, his comradely attitude, his personality, his originality, even when one had not yet learned of his other characteristics and unique virtues.

In those first days he was our troop doctor, and so the bonds of friendship and warm feelings for him were ever increasing. He was filled with a profound spirit of hatred and contempt for imperialism, not only because his political education was already considerably developed, but also because, shortly before, he had had the opportunity of witnessing the criminal imperialist intervention in Guatemala through the mercenaries who aborted the revolution in that country.

A person like Che did not require elaborate arguments. It was sufficient for him to know Cuba was in a similar situation and that there were people determined to struggle against that situation, arms in hand. It was sufficient for him to know that those people were inspired by genuinely revolutionary and patriotic ideals. That was more than enough.

One day, at the end of November 1956, he set out on the expedition toward Cuba with us. I recall that the trip was very hard for him, since, because of the circumstances under which it was necessary to organize the departure, he could not even provide himself with the medicine he needed. Throughout the trip, he suffered from a severe attack of asthma, with nothing to alleviate it, but also without ever complaining.

We arrived, set out on our first march, suffered our first setback, and at the end of some weeks, as you all know, a group of those *Granma* expeditionaries who had survived was able to reunite. Che continued to be the doctor of our group.

We came through the first battle victorious, and Che was already a soldier of our troop; at the same time he was still our doctor. We came through the second victorious battle and Che was not only a soldier, but the most outstanding soldier in that battle, carrying out for the first time one of those singular feats that characterized him in all military action. Our forces continued to develop and we soon faced another battle of extraordinary importance.

The situation was difficult. The information we had was erroneous in many respects. We were going to attack in full daylight — at dawn — a strongly defended, well-armed position at the edge of the sea. Enemy troops were at our rear, not very far, and in that confused situation it was necessary to ask people to make a supreme effort.

Comrade Juan Almeida had taken on one of the most difficult missions, but one of the flanks remained completely without forces — one of the flanks was left without an attacking force, placing the operation in danger. At that moment, Che, who was still functioning as our doctor, asked for three or four men, among them one with a machine gun, and in a matter of seconds set off rapidly to assume the mission of attack from that direction.

On that occasion he was not only an outstanding combatant but also an outstanding doctor, attending the wounded comrades and, at the same time, attending the wounded enemy soldiers.

After all the weapons had been captured and it became necessary to abandon that position, undertaking a long return march under the harassment of various enemy forces, someone had to stay behind with the wounded, and it was Che who did so. Aided by a small group of our soldiers, he took care of them, saved their lives, and later rejoined the column with them.

From that time onward, he stood out as a capable and valiant leader, one of those who, when a difficult mission is pending, do not wait to be asked to carry it out.

Thus it was at the battle of El Uvero. But he acted in a similar way on a previously unmentioned occasion during the first days when, following a betrayal, our little troop was attacked by surprise by a number of planes and we were forced to retreat under the bombardment. We had already walked a distance when we remembered some rifles of some peasant soldiers who had been with us in the first actions and had then asked permission to visit their families, at a time when there was still not much discipline in our embryonic army. At that moment, we thought the rifles might have to be given up for lost. But I recall it took no more than simply raising the problem for Che, despite the bombing, to volunteer, and having done so, quickly go to recover those rifles.

This was one of his principal characteristics: his willingness to instantly volunteer for the most dangerous mission. And naturally this aroused admiration — and twice the usual admiration, for a fellow combatant fighting alongside us who had not been born here, a person of profound ideas, a person in whose mind stirred the dream of struggle in other parts of the continent and who nonetheless was so altruistic, so selfless, so willing to always do the most difficult things, to constantly risk his life.

That was how he won the rank of commander and leader of the second column, organized in the Sierra Maestra. Thus his standing began to increase. He began to develop as a magnificent combatant who was to reach the highest ranks in the course of the war.

Che was an incomparable soldier. Che was an incomparable

leader. Che was, from a military point of view, an extraordinarily capable person, extraordinarily courageous, extraordinarily aggressive. If, as a guerrilla, he had his Achilles' heel, it was this excessively aggressive quality, his absolute contempt for danger.

The enemy believes it can draw certain conclusions from his death. Che was a master of warfare! He was an artist of guerrilla struggle! And he showed that an infinite number of times. But he showed it especially in two extraordinary deeds. One of these was the invasion, in which he led a column, a column pursued by thousands of enemy soldiers over flat and absolutely unknown terrain, carrying out — together with Camilo [Cienfuegos] — an extraordinary military accomplishment. He also showed it in his lightning campaign in Las Villas Province, especially in the audacious attack on the city of Santa Clara, entering — with a column of barely 300 men — a city defended by tanks, artillery, and several thousand infantry soldiers. Those two heroic deeds stamped him as an extraordinarily capable leader, as a master, as an artist of revolutionary war.

However, now after his heroic and glorious death, some people attempt to deny the truth or value of his concepts, his guerrilla theories. The artist may die — especially when he is an artist in a field as dangerous as revolutionary struggle — but what will surely never die is the art to which he dedicated his life, the art to which he dedicated his intelligence.

What is so strange about the fact that this artist died in combat? What is stranger is that he did not die in combat on one of the innumerable occasions when he risked his life during our revolutionary struggle. Many times it was necessary to take steps to keep him from losing his life in actions of minor significance.

And so it was in combat — in one of the many battles he fought — that he lost his life. We do not have sufficient evidence to enable us to deduce what circumstances preceded that combat, or how far he may have acted in an excessively aggressive way. But, we repeat, if as a guerrilla he had an Achilles' heel, it was his excessive aggressiveness, his absolute contempt for danger.

And this is where we can hardly agree with him, since we consider that his life, his experience, his capacity as a seasoned leader, his authority, and everything his life signified, were more valuable, incomparably more valuable than he himself, perhaps, believed.

His conduct may have been profoundly influenced by the

idea that people have a relative value in history, the idea that causes are not defeated when people fall, that the powerful march of history cannot and will not be halted when leaders fall.

That is true, there is no doubt about it. It shows his faith in people, his faith in ideas, his faith in examples. However — as I said a few days ago — with all our heart we would have liked to see him as a forger of victories, to see victories forged under his command, under his leadership, since people of his experience, of his caliber, of his really unique capacity, are not common.

We fully appreciate the value of his example. We are absolutely convinced that many people will strive to live up to his example, that people like him will emerge.

It is not easy to find a person with all the virtues that were combined in Che. It is not easy for a person, spontaneously, to develop a character like his. I would say that he is one of those people who are difficult to match and virtually impossible to surpass. But I would also say that the example of people like him contributes to the appearance of people of the same caliber.

In Che, we admire not only the fighter, the person capable of performing great feats. What he did, what he was doing, the very fact of his rising with a handful of men against the army of the oligarchy, trained by Yankee advisers sent in by Yankee imperialism, backed by the oligarchies of all neighboring countries — that in itself constitutes an extraordinary feat.

If we search the pages of history, it is likely that we will find no other case in which a leader with such a limited number of men has set about a task of such importance; a case in which a leader with such a limited number of men has set out to fight against such large forces. Such proof of confidence in himself, such proof of confidence in the peoples, such proof of faith in man's capacity to fight, can be looked for in the pages of history — but the likes of it will never be found.

And he fell.

The enemy believes it has defeated his ideas, his guerrilla concepts, his point of view on revolutionary armed struggle. What they accomplished, by a stroke of luck, was to eliminate him physically. What they accomplished was to gain an accidental advantage that an enemy may gain in war. We do not know to what degree that stroke of luck, that stroke of fortune, was helped along, in a battle like many others, by that characteristic of which we spoke before: his excessive aggressiveness, his absolute disdain for danger.

This also happened in our war of independence. In a battle at Dos Ríos they killed [José Martí] the apostle of our independence; in a battle at Punta Brava, they killed Antonio Maceo, a veteran of hundreds of battles [in the Cuban war of independence]. Countless leaders, countless patriots of our war of independence were killed in similar battles. Nevertheless, that did not spell defeat for the Cuban cause.

The death of Che — as we said a few days ago — is a hard blow, a tremendous blow for the revolutionary movement because it deprives it, without a doubt, of its most experienced and able leader.

But those who boast of victory are mistaken. They are mistaken when they think that his death is the end of his ideas, the end of his tactics, the end of his guerrilla concepts, the end of his theory. For the person who fell, as a mortal person, as a person who faced bullets time and again, as a soldier, as a leader, was a thousand times more able than those who killed him by a stroke of luck.

However, how should revolutionaries face this serious setback? How should they face this loss? If Che had to express an opinion on this point, what would it be? He gave this opinion, he expressed this opinion quite clearly when he wrote in his message to the [Tricontinental] Latin American Solidarity Conference that if death surprised him anywhere, it would be welcome as long as his battle cry had reached a receptive ear and another hand reached out to take up his rifle.

His battle cry will reach not just one receptive ear, but millions of receptive ears! And not one hand but millions of hands, inspired by his example, will reach out to take up arms! New leaders will emerge. The people of the receptive ears and the outstretched hands will need leaders who emerge from their ranks, just as leaders have emerged in all revolutions.

Those hands will not have available a leader of Che's extraordinary experience and enormous ability. Those leaders will be formed in the process of struggle. Those leaders will emerge from among the millions of receptive ears, from the millions of hands that will sooner or later reach out to take up arms.

It is not that we feel that his death will necessarily have immediate repercussions in the practical sphere of revolutionary struggle, that his death will necessarily have immediate repercussions in the practical sphere of development of this struggle. The fact is that when Che took up arms again he was not thinking of an immediate victory; he was not thinking of a speedy victory against the forces of the oligarchies and imperialism. As an experienced fighter, he was prepared for a prolonged struggle of 5, 10, 15, or 20 years, if necessary. He was ready to fight 5, 10, 15, or 20 years, or all his life if need be! And within that perspective, his death — or rather his example — will have tremendous repercussions. The force of that example will be invincible.

Those who attach significance to the lucky blow that struck Che down try in vain to deny his experience and his capacity as a leader. Che was an extraordinarily able military leader. But when we remember Che, when we think of Che, we do not think fundamentally of his military virtues. No! Warfare is a means and not an end. Warfare is a tool of revolutionaries. The important thing is the revolution. The important thing is the revolutionary cause, revolutionary ideas, revolutionary objectives, revolutionary sentiments, revolutionary virtues!

And it is in that field, in the field of ideas, in the field of sentiments, in the field of revolutionary virtues, in the field of intelligence, that — apart from his military virtues — we feel the tremendous loss that his death means to the revolutionary movement.

Che's extraordinary character was made up of virtues that are rarely found together. He stood out as an unsurpassed person of action, but Che was not only that — he was also a person of visionary intelligence and broad culture, a profound thinker. That is, the man of ideas and the man of action were combined within him.

But it is not only that Che possessed the double characteristic of the man of ideas — of profound ideas — and the man of action, but that Che as a revolutionary united in himself the virtues that can be defined as the fullest expression of the virtues of a revolutionary: a person of total integrity, a person of supreme sense of honor, of absolute sincerity, a person of stoic and Spartan living habits, a person in whose conduct not one stain can be found. He constituted, through his virtues, what can be called a truly model revolutionary.

When people die it is usual to make speeches, to emphasize their virtues. But rarely can one say of a person with greater justice, with greater accuracy, what we say of Che on this occasion: that he was a pure example of revolutionary virtues!

But he possessed another quality, not a quality of the intellect nor of the will, not a quality derived from experience, from struggle, but a quality of the heart: he was an extraordinarily human being, extraordinarily sensitive!

That is why we say, when we think of his life, when we think of his conduct, that he constituted the singular case of a most extraordinary human, able to unite in his personality not only the characteristics of the man of action, but also of the man of thought, of the person of immaculate revolutionary virtues and of extraordinary human sensibility, joined with an iron character, a will of steel, indomitable tenacity.

Because of this, he has left to the future generations not only his experience, his knowledge as an outstanding soldier, but also, at the same time, the fruits of his intelligence. He wrote with the virtuosity of a master of our language. His narratives of the war are incomparable. The depth of his thinking is impressive. He never wrote about anything with less than extraordinary seriousness, with less than extraordinary profundity — and we have no doubt that some of his writings will pass on to posterity as classic documents of revolutionary thought.

Thus, as fruits of that vigorous and profound intelligence, he left us countless memories, countless narratives that, without his work, without his efforts, might have been lost forever.

An indefatigable worker, during the years that he served our country he did not know a single day of rest. Many were the responsibilities assigned to him: as president of the National Bank, as director of the Central Planning Board, as minister of industry, as commander of military regions, as the head of political or economic or fraternal delegations.

His versatile intelligence was able to undertake with maximum assurance any task of any kind. Thus he brilliantly represented our country in numerous international conferences, just as he brilliantly led soldiers in combat, just as he was a model worker in charge of any of the institutions he was assigned to. And for him there were no days of rest; for him there were no hours of rest!

If we looked through the windows of his offices, he had the lights on all hours of the night, studying, or rather, working or studying. For he was a student of all problems; he was a tireless reader. His thirst for learning was practically insatiable, and the hours he stole from sleep he devoted to study.

He devoted his scheduled days off to voluntary work. He was the inspiration and provided the greatest incentive for the work that is today carried out by hundreds of thousands of people throughout the country. He stimulated that activity in which our people are making greater and greater efforts.

As a revolutionary, as a communist revolutionary, a true communist, he had a boundless faith in moral values. He had a boundless faith in the consciousness of human beings. And we should say that he saw, with absolute clarity, the moral impulse as the fundamental lever in the construction of communism in human society.

He thought, developed, and wrote many things. And on a day like today it should be stated that Che's writings, Che's political and revolutionary thought, will be of permanent value to the Cuban revolutionary process and to the Latin American revolutionary process. And we do not doubt that his ideas — as a man of action, as a man of thought, as a person of untarnished moral virtues, as a person of unexcelled human sensitivity, as a person of spotless conduct — have and will continue to have universal value.

The imperialists boast of their triumph at having killed this guerrilla fighter in action. The imperialists boast of a triumphant stroke of luck that led to the elimination of such a formidable man of action. But perhaps the imperialists do not know or pretend not to know that the man of action was only one of the many facets of the personality of that combatant. And if we speak of sorrow, we are saddened not only at having lost a person of action. We are saddened at having lost a person of virtue. We are saddened at having lost a person of unsurpassed human sensitivity. We are saddened at having lost such a mind. We are saddened to think that he was only 39 years old at the time of his death. We are saddened at missing the additional fruits that we would have received from that intelligence and that ever richer experience.

We have an idea of the dimension of the loss for the revolutionary movement. However, here is the weak side of the imperialist enemy: they think that by eliminating a person physically they have eliminated his thinking — that by eliminating him physically they have eliminated his ideas, eliminated his virtues, eliminated his example.

So shameless are they in this belief that they have no hesitation in publishing, as the most natural thing in the world, the by now almost universally accepted circumstances in which they murdered him after he had been seriously wounded in action. They do not even seem aware of the repugnance of the procedure, of the shamelessness of the acknowledgement. They have published it as if thugs, oligarchs, and mercenaries had the right to shoot a seriously wounded revolutionary combatant.

Even worse, they explain why they did it. They assert that Che's trial would have been quite an earthshaker, that it would have been impossible to place this revolutionary in the dock.

And not only that, they have not hesitated to spirit away his remains. Be it true or false, they certainly announced they had cremated his body, thus beginning to show their fear, beginning to show that they are not so sure that by physically eliminating the combatant, they can eliminate his ideas, eliminate his example.

Che died defending no other interest, no other cause than the cause of the exploited and the oppressed of this continent. Che died defending no other cause than the cause of the poor and the humble of this earth. And the exemplary manner and the selflessness with which he defended that cause cannot be disputed even by his most bitter enemies.

Before history, people who act as he did, people who do and give everything for the cause of the poor, grow in stature with each passing day and find a deeper place in the heart of the peoples with each passing day. The imperialist enemies are beginning to see this, and it will not be long before it will be proved that his death will, in the long run, be like a seed that will give rise to many people determined to imitate him, many people determined to follow his example.

We are absolutely convinced that the revolutionary cause on this continent will recover from the blow, that the revolutionary movement on this continent will not be crushed by this blow.

From the revolutionary point of view, from the point of view of our people, how should we view Che's example? Do we feel we have lost him? It is true that we will not see new writings of his. It is true that we will never again hear his voice. But Che has left a heritage to the world, a great heritage, and we who knew him so well can become in large measure his beneficiaries.

He left us his revolutionary thinking, his revolutionary virtues. He left us his character, his will, his tenacity, his spirit of work. In a word, he left us his example! And Che's example will be a model for our people. Che's example will be the ideal model for our people!

If we wish to express what we expect our revolutionary combatants, our militants, our people to be, we must say, without hesitation: let them be like Che! If we wish to express what we want the people of future generations to be, we must say: let them be like Che! If we wish to say how we want our children to be educated, we must say without hesitation: we want them to be educated in Che's spirit! If we want the model of a person, the model of a human being who does not belong to our time but to the future, I say from the depths of my heart that such a model, without a single stain on his conduct, without a single stain on his action, without a single stain on his behavior, is Che! If we wish to express what we want our children to be, we must say from our very hearts as ardent revolutionaries: we want them to be like Che!

Che has become a model of what future humans should be, not only for our people but also for people everywhere in Latin America. Che carried to its highest expression revolutionary stoicism, the revolutionary spirit of sacrifice, revolutionary combativeness, the revolutionary's spirit of work. Che brought the ideas of Marxism-Leninism to their freshest, purest, most revolutionary expression. No other person of our time has carried the spirit of proletarian internationalism to its highest possible level as Che did.

And when one speaks of a proletarian internationalist, and when an example of a proletarian internationalist is sought, that example, high above any other, will be the example of Che. National flags, prejudices, chauvinism, and egoism had disappeared from his mind and heart. He was ready to shed his generous blood spontaneously and immediately, on behalf of any people, for the cause of any people!

Thus, his blood fell on our soil when he was wounded in several battles, and his blood was shed in Bolivia, for the liberation of the exploited and the oppressed, of the humble and the poor. That blood was shed for the sake of all the exploited and all the oppressed. That blood was shed for all the peoples of the Americas and for the people of Vietnam — because while fighting there in Bolivia, fighting against the oligarchies and imperialism, he knew that he was offering Vietnam the highest possible expression of his solidarity!

It is for this reason, comrades of the revolution, that we must face the future with firmness and determination, with optimism. And in Che's example, we will always look for inspiration — inspiration in struggle, inspiration in tenacity, inspiration in intransigence toward the enemy, inspiration in internationalist feeling!

Therefore, after tonight's moving ceremony, after this incredible demonstration of vast popular recognition — incredible for its magnitude, discipline, and spirit of devotion — which demonstrates that our people are a sensitive, grateful people who know how to honor the memory of the brave who die in combat, that our people recognize those who serve them; which demonstrates the people's solidarity with the revolutionary struggle and how this people will raise aloft and maintain ever higher aloft revolutionary banners and revolutionary principles — today, in these moments of remembrance, let us lift our spirits and, with optimism in the future, with absolute optimism in the final victory of the peoples, say to Che and to the heroes who fought and died with him:

Hasta la victoria siempre! [Ever onward to victory]

Patria o muerte! [Homeland or death]

Venceremos! [We will win]

Chapter four

The diary kept by Che Guevara during the guerrilla campaign in Bolivia was confiscated following his capture on October 8, 1967. Journalists were able to photograph several pages of it and copies were made for the Pentagon and CIA. The Bolivian regime then pursued efforts to sell the publication rights — which they claimed belonged to them as a war trophy — for $300,000 or more. These plans were short-lived, however, when the Cuban government obtained photocopies of the diary from Bolivia's Minister of the Interior, Antonio Arguedas. When his role in this became known, Arguedas was forced to flee the country.

Before proceeding with its publication, the Cuban government conducted a rigorous check of the manuscript to verify its authenticity. This process was aided by three Cuban survivors of the campaign, who had escaped the army's ambush and made their way through the Andes to Chile on foot. On July 1, 1968, the diary was published and distributed free of charge to the people of Cuba. Arrangements were also made for its translation and publication in a number of other countries. An English version appeared in Ramparts *magazine in a special edition of more than 200,000 copies.*

In claiming that the diary was not genuine, Bolivian President Barrientos called it a "fictitious diary, falsified." Castro responded that Cuba was willing to provide reproductions of the microfilm to the international press so they could be checked against the original diary, if the Bolivian government would permit that to be done.

The following is Fidel Castro's introduction to the 1968 edition of the diary.

IT WAS CHE'S CUSTOM during his days as a guerrilla [during the Cuban revolutionary war] to carefully record his daily observations in a personal diary. During long marches over rugged and difficult terrain, in the midst of damp woods, when the lines of men, always hunched over from the weight of their packs, ammunition, and weapons, would stop for a moment to rest, or when the column would receive orders to halt and set up camp at the end of an exhausting day's march, you would see Che — as he was from the beginning affectionately nicknamed by the Cubans — take out a small notebook and, with the tiny and nearly illegible handwriting of a doctor, write his notes.

What he was able to save from these notes he later used in writing his magnificent historical narratives of the revolutionary war in Cuba — accounts full of revolutionary, educational, and human content.

This time, thanks to his invariable habit of noting the main events of each day, we have at our disposal rigorously exact, priceless, and detailed information on the heroic final months of his life in Bolivia.

These notes, not really written for publication, served as a tool in the constant evaluation of events, situations, and people. They also served as an outlet for the expression of his keenly observant and analytical spirit, often laced with a fine sense of humor. They are soberly written and form a coherent whole from beginning to end.

It should be kept in mind that they were written during those rare moments of rest in the middle of an heroic and superhuman physical effort. Also to be remembered are his exhausting obligations as leader of a guerrilla detachment in the difficult first stages of a struggle of this nature, which unfolded under incredibly harsh material conditions. This reveals once more his way of working, his will of steel.

The diary, in the course of analyzing in detail the incidents of each day, takes note of the shortcomings, critical assessments, and recriminations that are part of and inevitable in the development of a revolutionary guerrilla struggle.

Inside a guerrilla detachment such assessments must take place incessantly. This is especially true in the stage in which it consists of a small nucleus facing extremely adverse material conditions and an enemy infinitely superior in number, when the slightest negligence or the most insignificant mistake can be fatal. The leader must be extremely demanding. He must use each event or episode, no matter how insignificant it may seem, to educate the combatants and future cadres of new guerrilla detachments.

The process of training a guerrilla force is a constant appeal to each man's consciousness and honor. Che knew how to touch the most sensitive fibers in revolutionaries. When Marcos, after being repeatedly admonished by Che, was warned that he could be dishonorably discharged from the guerrilla unit, he replied, "I would rather be shot!" Later he gave his life heroically. Similar behavior could be noted among all those Che placed confidence in and whom he had to admonish for one reason or another in the course of the struggle. He was a fraternal and humane leader, but he also knew how to be demanding and, at times, severe. But above all, and even more so than with the others, Che was severe with himself. He based discipline on the guerrilla's moral consciousness and on the tremendous force of his own example.

The diary also contains numerous references to [Régis] Debray. It reflects the enormous concern Che felt over the arrest and imprisonment of the revolutionary writer who had been given a mission to carry out in Europe — although at heart Che would have preferred him to have stayed with the guerrilla unit. That is why Che shows a certain lack of patience and, on occasion, some doubts about his behavior.

Che had no way of knowing the odyssey Debray lived through in the hands of the repressive forces, or the firm and courageous attitude he maintained in face of his captors and torturers. He noted, however, the enormous political significance of the trial and on October 3, six days before his death, in the middle of bitter and tense events, he wrote: "We heard an interview with Debray, very courageous when faced with a student provocateur." That was his last reference to the writer.

The Cuban revolution and its relation to the guerrilla movement are repeatedly referred to in the diary. Some may interpret our decision to publish it as an act of provocation that will give the enemies of the revolution — the Yankee imperialists and their allies, the Latin American oligarchs — arguments for redoubling their efforts to blockade, isolate, and attack Cuba.

Those who judge the facts this way should remember that Yankee imperialism has never needed a pretext to carry out its crimes anywhere in the world, and that its efforts to crush the Cuban revolution began as soon as our country passed its first revolutionary law. This stems from the obvious and well-known fact that imperialism is the policeman of world reaction, the systematic supporter of counterrevolution, and the protector of the most backward and inhuman social structures that remain in the world.

Solidarity with a revolutionary movement may be taken as a pretext for Yankee aggression, but it will never be the real cause. To deny solidarity in order to avoid giving a pretext is a ridiculous, ostrich-like policy that has nothing to do with the internationalist character of the social revolutions of today. To abandon solidarity with a revolutionary movement not only does not avoid providing a pretext, but in effect serves to show solidarity with Yankee imperialism and its policy of dominating and enslaving the world.

Cuba is a small country, economically underdeveloped as are countries dominated and exploited for centuries by colonialism and imperialism. It is located only 90 miles from the coast of the United States, has a Yankee naval base on its territory [Guantánamo], and faces numerous obstacles in attaining socio-economic development. Grave dangers have threatened our country since the triumph of the revolution. But imperialism will never make us yield for these reasons, because the difficulties that flow from a consistently revolutionary line of action are of no importance to us.

From the revolutionary point of view, there is no alternative but to publish Che's Bolivian diary. It fell into the hands of [René] Barrientos, who immediately sent copies to the CIA, the Pentagon, and the U.S. government. Journalists connected with the CIA had access to the document inside Bolivia. Having made photocopies of it, they promised that they would refrain, for the moment, from publishing it.

The Barrientos government and the top-ranking military officers have more than enough reasons not to publish the diary. It reveals the immense incapacity of their army and the countless defeats they were dealt by a handful of determined guerrillas who, in a matter of weeks, took nearly 200 weapons from them in combat. Furthermore, Che describes Barrientos and his regime in terms they deserve, with words that cannot be erased from history.

Imperialism also had its own reasons. Che and the extraordinary example he set are gaining increasing force in the world. His ideas, image, and name are banners of struggle against the injustices suffered by the oppressed and exploited. They evoke impassioned interest among students and intellectuals the world over.

In the United States itself the Black movement and

progressive students, both of which are continuing to grow in numbers, have made Che's figure their own. In the most combative demonstrations for civil rights and against the aggression in Vietnam, his image is brandished as a symbol of struggle. Few times in history, perhaps never before, has a figure, a name, an example become a universal symbol so quickly and with such impassioned force. This is because Che embodies, in its purest and most selfless form, the internationalist spirit that marks the world of today and that will characterize even more the world of tomorrow.

Out of a continent yesterday oppressed by colonial powers, today exploited and held in backwardness and the most iniquitous underdevelopment by Yankee imperialism, there has emerged this singular figure who has become the universal symbol of revolutionary struggle, even in the metropolitan centers of the imperialists and colonialists.

The Yankee imperialists fear the power of this example and everything that may help to spread it. The diary is the living expression of an extraordinary personality; a lesson in guerrilla warfare written in the heat and tension of daily events, as flammable as gunpowder; a demonstration in life that the people of Latin America are not powerless in face of the enslavers of entire peoples and of their mercenary armies. That is its intrinsic value, and that is what has kept them from publishing it up until now.

Also among those who may be interested in keeping the diary unpublished are the pseudorevolutionaries, opportunists, and charlatans of every stripe. These people call themselves Marxists, communists, and other such titles. They have not, however, hesitated to call Che a mistaken adventurer or, when they speak more benignly, an idealist whose death marked the swan song of revolutionary armed struggle in Latin America. "If Che himself," they say, "the greatest exponent of these ideas and an experienced guerrilla fighter, died in the guerrilla struggle and his movement failed to free Bolivia, it only shows how mistaken he was...!" How many of these miserable creatures were happy with the death of Che and have not even blushed at the thought that their positions and reasoning completely coincide with those of imperialism and the most reactionary oligarchs!

That is how they justify themselves. That is how they justify their treacherous leaders who, at a given moment, did not hesitate to play at armed struggle with the underlying intention — as could be seen later — of destroying the guerrilla detachments, putting the brakes on revolutionary action, and imposing their own shameful and ridiculous political schemes, because they were absolutely incapable of carrying out any other line. That is how they justify those who do not want to fight, who will never fight for the people and their liberation. That is how they justify those who have made a caricature of revolutionary ideas, turning them into an opium-like dogma with neither content nor message for the masses; those who have converted the organizations of popular struggle into instruments of conciliation with domestic and foreign exploiters; and those who advocate policies that have nothing to do with the genuine interests of the exploited peoples of this continent.

Che thought of his death as something natural and probable in the process. He made an effort to stress, especially in his last writings, that this eventuality would not hold back the inevitable march of the revolution in Latin America. In his Message to the Tricontinental, he reiterated this thought: "Our every action is a battle cry against imperialism.... Wherever death may surprise us, let it be welcome if our battle cry has reached even one receptive ear, if another hand reaches out to take up our arms."

Che considered himself a soldier in the revolution, with absolutely no concern as to whether he would survive it. Those who see the outcome of his struggle in Bolivia as marking the failure of his ideas can, with the same oversimplification, deny the validity of the ideas and struggles of all the great revolutionary precursors and thinkers. This includes the founders of Marxism, who were themselves unable to complete the task and to view in life the fruits of their noble efforts.

In Cuba, Martí and Maceo were killed in combat; Yankee intervention followed, ending the war of independence and frustrating the immediate objectives of their struggle. Brilliant advocates of socialist revolution like Julio Antonio Mella have been killed, murdered by agents in the service of imperialism. But these deaths could not, in the long run, block the triumph of a process that began 100 years ago. And absolutely nothing can call into question the profound justice of the cause and line of struggle of those eminent fighters, nor the timeliness of their basic ideas, which have always inspired Cuban revolutionaries.

In Che's diary, from the notes he wrote, you can see how real the possibilities of success were, how extraordinary the catalyzing power of the guerrilla struggle. On one occasion, in face of evident signs of the Bolivian regime's weakness and rapid deterioration, he wrote: "The government is disintegrating rapidly. It's a shame we don't have 100 more men right now."

Che knew from his experience in Cuba how often our small guerrilla detachment had been on the verge of being wiped out. Whether such things happen depends almost entirely on chance and the imponderables of war. But would such an eventuality have given anyone the right to consider our line erroneous, and in addition to take it as an example to discourage revolution and inculcate a sense of powerlessness among the peoples? Many times in history revolutionary processes have been preceded by adverse episodes. We ourselves in Cuba, didn't we have the experience of Moncada just six years before the definitive triumph of the people's armed struggle?

From July 26, 1953 — the attack on the Moncada garrison in Santiago de Cuba — to December 2, 1956 — the landing of the *Granma* — revolutionary struggle in Cuba in face of a modern, well-equipped army seemed to many people to lack any prospect for success. The action of a handful of fighters was seen as a chimera of idealists and dreamers "who were deeply mistaken." The crushing defeat and total dispersal of the inexperienced guerrilla detachment on December 5, 1956, seemed to confirm entirely those pessimistic forebodings. But only 25 months later the remnants of that guerrilla unit had already developed the strength and experience necessary to annihilate that same army.

In all epochs and under all circumstances, there will always be an abundance of pretexts for not fighting; but not fighting is the only way to never attain freedom. Che did not live as long as his ideas; he fertilized them with his blood. It is certain, on the other hand, that his pseudorevolutionary critics, with all their political cowardice and eternal lack of action, will outlive by far the evidence of their own stupidity.

To be noted, as can be seen in the diary, are the actions of one of those revolutionary specimens that are becoming typical in Latin America these days. Mario Monje, brandishing the title of secretary of the Communist Party of Bolivia, sought to dispute with Che the political and military leadership of the movement. Monje claimed, moreover, that he had intended to resign his party post to take on this responsibility; in his opinion, obviously, it was enough to have once held that title to claim such a prerogative.

Mario Monje, naturally, had no experience in guerrilla warfare and had never been in combat. In addition, the fact that he considered himself a communist should at least have obliged him to dispense with the gross and mundane chauvinism that had already been overcome by those who fought for Bolivia's first independence.

With such a conception of what an anti-imperialist struggle on this continent should be, "communist leaders" of this type do not even surpass the level of internationalism of the aboriginal tribes subjugated by the European colonizers in the epoch of the conquest.

Bolivia and its historical capital, Sucre, were named after the country's first liberators [Simon Bolívar and Antonio José de Sucre], both of whom were Venezuelan. And in this country, in a struggle for the definitive liberation of his people, the leader of the Communist Party had the possibility of enlisting the cooperation of the political, organizational, and military talent of a genuine revolutionary titan, of a person whose cause was not limited by the narrow and artificial — not to mention unjust — borders of Bolivia. Yet he did nothing but engage in disgraceful, ridiculous, and unmerited claims to leadership.

Bolivia does not have an outlet to the sea. For its own liberation, to avoid exposure to a cruel blockade, it more than any other country needs revolutionary victories by its neighbors. Che, because of his enormous authority, ability, and experience, was the person who could have accelerated this process.

In the period before a split occurred in the Bolivian Communist Party, Che had established relations with leaders and members of it, soliciting their help for the revolutionary movement in South America. Under authorization from the party, some members worked with Che for years on various assignments. When the split occurred, it created a special situation, given that a number of the people who had been working with him ended up in one or another group. But Che did not see the struggle in Bolivia as an isolated occurrence, rather as part of a revolutionary liberation movement that would soon extend to other countries in South America. He sought to organize a movement free of sectarianism, one that could be joined by anyone who wanted to fight for the liberation of Bolivia and of all the other peoples of Latin America subjugated by imperialism.

In the initial phase of preparing a base for the guerrilla unit, however, Che depended for the most part on the help of a group of courageous and discreet collaborators who, at the time of the split, remained in the party headed by Monje. Although he certainly felt no sympathy toward Monje, in deference to them he invited Monje to visit his camp first. He then invited Moises Guevara, a leader of the miners and a political leader. Moises Guevara had left the party to join in the formation of another organization, the one led by Oscar Zamora. He later left that group as well because of differences with Zamora. Zamora was another Monje. He had once promised Che he would help in organizing the armed guerrilla struggle in Bolivia. He later backed away from that commitment and cowardly folded his arms at the hour of action. After Che's death, Zamora became one of his most venomous "Marxist-Leninist" critics. Moises Guevara joined Che without hesitation, as he had sought to do long before Che arrived in Bolivia. He offered his support and gave his life heroically for the revolutionary cause.

The group of Bolivian guerrillas who until then had stayed with Monje's organization also joined Che. Led by Inti and Coco Peredo, who proved to be courageous, outstanding fighters, they left Monje and decisively backed Che. But Monje, seeking revenge, began to sabotage the movement. In La Paz he intercepted well-trained communist militants who were on their way to join the guerrillas. These facts demonstrate that within the ranks of revolutionaries, men who meet all the conditions necessary for struggle can be criminally frustrated in their development by incapable, maneuvering, and charlatan-like leaders.

Che was a person never personally interested in posts, leadership, or honors. But he believed revolutionary guerrilla warfare was the fundamental form of action for the liberation of the peoples of Latin America, given the economic, political, and social situation of nearly all Latin American countries. And he was firmly convinced that the military and political leadership of the guerrilla struggle had to be unified. He also believed the struggle could be led only from the guerrilla unit itself, and not from the comfortable offices of bureaucrats in the cities. So he was not prepared to give up leadership of a guerrilla nucleus that, at a later stage of its development, was intended to develop into a struggle of broad dimensions in Latin America. And he certainly was not prepared to turn over such leadership to an inexperienced emptyhead with narrow chauvinist views. Such chauvinism often infects even revolutionary elements of various countries in Latin America. Che believed that it must be fought because it represents reactionary, ridiculous, and sterile thinking.

"And let us develop genuine proletarian internationalism...." he said in his Message to the Tricontinental. "Let the flag under which we fight be the sacred cause of the liberation of humanity, so that to die under the colors of Vietnam, Venezuela, Guatemala, Laos, Guinea, Colombia, Bolivia... to mention only the current scenes of armed struggle, will be equally glorious and desirable for a Latin American, an Asian, an African, and even a European.

"Every drop of blood spilled in a land under whose flag one was not born is experience gathered by the survivor to be applied later in the struggle for liberation of one's own country. And every people that liberates itself is a step in the battle for the liberation of one's own people."

In the same way, Che believed fighters from various Latin American countries would participate in the guerrilla detachment, that the guerrilla struggle in Bolivia would be a school in which revolutionaries would serve their apprenticeship in combat. To help him with this task he wanted to have, together with the Bolivians, a small nucleus of experienced guerrilla fighters, nearly all of whom had been comrades of his in the Sierra Maestra during the revolutionary struggle in Cuba. These were men whose abilities, courage, and spirit of self-sacrifice were known by Che. None of them hesitated to respond to his call, none of them abandoned him, none of them surrendered.

In the Bolivian campaign Che acted with his proverbial tenacity, skill, stoicism, and exemplary attitude. It might be said that he was consumed with the importance of the mission he had assigned himself, and at all times he proceeded with a spirit of irreproachable responsibility. When the guerrilla unit committed an error of carelessness, he quickly called attention to it, corrected it, and noted it in his diary.

Adverse factors built up against him unbelievably. One example was the separation — supposed to last for just a few days — of part of the guerrilla detachment. That unit included a courageous group of men, some of them sick or convalescent.

Once contact between the two groups was lost in very rough terrain, separation continued, and for endless months Che was occupied with the effort to find them. In this period his asthma — an ailment easily treated with simple medication, but one that, lacking the medication, became a terrible enemy — attacked him relentlessly. It became a serious problem since the medical supplies that had been accumulated by the guerrillas beforehand had been discovered and captured by the enemy. This fact, along with the annihilation at the end of August of the part of the guerrilla detachment he had lost contact with, were factors that weighed considerably in the development of events. But Che, with his iron will, overcame his physical difficulties and never for an instant cut back his activity or let his spirits fall.

Che had many contacts with the Bolivian peasants. Their character — highly suspicious and cautious — would have come as no surprise to Che, who knew their mentality perfectly well because he had dealt with them on other occasions. He knew that winning them over to the cause required long, arduous, and patient work, but he had no doubt that in the long run they would obtain the support of the peasants.

If we follow the thread of events carefully, it becomes clear that even when the number of men on whom Che could count was quite small — in the month of September, a few weeks before his death — the guerrilla unit still retained its capacity to develop. It also still had a few Bolivian cadres, such as the brothers Inti and Coco Peredo, who were already beginning to show magnificent leadership potential.

It was the ambush in Higueras [on September 26, 1967] — the sole successful action by the army against the detachment led by Che — that created a situation they could not overcome. In that ambush, in broad daylight, the advance guard was killed and several more men were wounded as they headed toward a peasant area with a higher level of political development — an objective that does not appear to have been noted in the diary but that was known to the survivors. It was without doubt dangerous to advance by daylight along the same route they had been following for days, with inevitably broad contact with the residents of an area they were crossing for the first time. It was obvious and certain that the army would intercept them at some point. But Che, fully conscious of this, decided to run the risk in order to help the doctor [Octavio de la Concepcion de la Pedreja

(Moro)], who was in very poor physical condition.

The day before the ambush, he wrote: "We reached Pujio but there were people who had seen us down below the day before, which means we are being announced ahead of time by Radio Bemba [word of mouth].... The march with mules is becoming dangerous, but I want the doctor to travel in the best possible way because he is very weak."

The following day he wrote: "At 13:00 the advance guard set out to try to reach Jagüey and to make a decision there about the mules and the doctor." That is, he was seeking a solution for the sick, so as to get off the road and take the necessary precautions. But that same afternoon, before the advance guard reached Jagüey, the fatal ambush occurred, leaving the detachment in an untenable situation.

A few days later, encircled in the El Yuro ravine, Che fought his final battle.

Recalling the feat carried out by this handful of revolutionaries touches one deeply. The struggle against the hostile natural environment in which their action took place constitutes by itself an insurmountable page of heroism. Never in history has so small a number of men set out on such a gigantic task. Their faith and absolute conviction that the immense revolutionary capacity of the peoples of Latin America could be awakened, their confidence in themselves and the determination with which they took on this objective — those things give us a just measure of these men.

One day Che said to the guerrilla fighters in Bolivia: "This type of struggle gives us the opportunity to become revolutionaries, the highest form of the human species, and it also enables us to become men. Those who cannot reach either of these two stages should say so and leave the struggle."

Those who fought with him until the end have become worthy of such honored terms. They symbolize the type of revolutionary and the type of person history is now calling on for a truly stubborn and difficult task — the revolutionary trans-formation of Latin America.

The enemy our forefathers faced in the first struggle for independence was a decadent colonial power. Revolutionaries of today have as their enemy the most powerful bulwark of the imperialist camp, equipped with the most modern technology and industry. This enemy not only organized and equipped a new army for Bolivia — where the people had destroyed the previous repressive military apparatus — and immediately sent weapons and advisers to help in the struggle against the guerrillas. It has also provided military and technical support on the same scale to every repressive force on the continent. And when these methods are not enough, it has intervened directly with its troops, as in the Dominican Republic.

Fighting this enemy requires the type of revolutionaries and men Che spoke of. Without this type of revolutionary and men, ready to do what they did; without the spirit to confront the enormous obstacles they faced; without the readiness to die that accompanied them at every moment; without their deeply held conviction in the justice of their cause and their unyielding faith in the invincible force of the peoples, against a power like Yankee imperialism, whose military, technical, and economic resources are felt throughout the entire world — without these, the liberation of the peoples of this continent will not be attained.

The people of the United States themselves are beginning to become aware that the monstrous political superstructure that reigns in their country has for some time no longer been the idyllic bourgeois republic the country's founders established nearly 200 years ago. They are increasingly subjected to the moral barbarism of an irrational, alienating, dehumanized, and brutal system that takes from the people of the United States a growing number of victims in its wars of aggression, its political crimes, its racial aberrations, the miserable hierarchy it has established for human beings, its repugnant waste of economic, scientific, and human resources on its enormous, reactionary, and repressive military apparatus — in the midst of a world where three-quarters of humanity lives in underdevelopment and hunger.

Only the revolutionary transformation of Latin America will enable the people of the United States to settle their own accounts with imperialism. At the same time, and in the same way, the growing struggle of the people of the United States against imperialist policy can become a decisive ally of the revolutionary movement in Latin America.

An enormous differentiation and imbalance occurred in the Americas at the beginning of this century. On one side a powerful and rapidly industrializing nation, in accordance with the very law of its social and economic dynamics, was marching toward imperial heights. On the other side, the weak and stagnant countries in the balkanized remainder of the Americas were kept under the boot of feudal oligarchies and their reactionary armies. If this part of the hemisphere does not undergo a profound revolutionary transformation, that earlier gap will seem but a pale reflection of not just the enormous present unevenness in finance, science, and technology, but rather of the horrible imbalance that, at an increasingly accelerated rate, the imperialist superstructure will impose on the peoples of Latin America in the next 20 years.

If we stay on this road, we will be increasingly poor, weak, dependent, and enslaved to imperialism. This gloomy perspective also confronts, to an equal degree, all the underdeveloped nations of Africa and Asia. If the industrialized and educated nations of Europe, with their Common Market and supranational scientific institutions, are worried about the possibility of being left behind and contemplate with fear the perspective of being converted into economic colonies of Yankee imperialism — what does the future have in store for the peoples of Latin America?

This is unquestionably the real situation that decisively affects the destiny of our peoples. What is urgently needed is a deep-going revolutionary transformation that can gather together all the moral, material, and human forces in this part of the world and launch them forward so as to overcome the economic, scientific, and technological backwardness of centuries; a backwardness that is greater still when compared with the industrialized world to which we are tributaries and will continue to be to an even greater degree, especially to the United States. If some liberal or bourgeois reformist, or some pseudorevolutionary charlatan, incapable of action, has a different answer; and if, in addition, he can provide the formula, the magic road to carrying it out, that is different from Che's conception; one that can sweep away the oligarchs, despots, and petty politicians — that is to say, the servants — and the Yankee monopolists — that is, the masters — and can do it with all the urgency the circumstances require; then let him stand up to challenge Che.

But no one really has an honest answer or a consistent policy that will bring genuine hope to the nearly 300 million human beings who make up the population of Latin America. Devastatingly poor in their overwhelming majority and increasing in number to 600 million within 25 years, they have the right to the material things of life, to culture, and to civilization. So the most dignified thing would be to remain silent in face of the action of Che and those who fell with him, courageously defending their ideas. The feat carried out by this handful of men, guided by the noble idea of redeeming a continent, will remain the greatest proof of what determination, heroism, and human greatness can accomplish. It is an example that will illuminate the consciousness and preside over the struggle of the peoples of Latin America. Che's heroic cry will reach the receptive ear of the poor and exploited for whom he gave his life; many hands will come forward to take up arms to win their definitive liberation.

On October 7, Che wrote his last lines. The following day, at 1:00 in the afternoon, in a narrow ravine where he proposed waiting until nightfall in order to break out of the encirclement, a large enemy force made contact with them. The small group of men who now made up the detachment fought heroically until dusk. From individual positions located on the bottom of the ravine, and on the top edges, they faced a mass of soldiers who surrounded and attacked them. There were no survivors among those who fought in the positions closest to Che. Since beside him were the doctor in the grave state of health mentioned before, and a Peruvian guerrilla who was also in very poor physical condition, everything seems to indicate that until he fell wounded, Che did his utmost to safeguard the withdrawal of these comrades to a safer place. The doctor was not killed in the same battle, but rather several days later at a place not far from the El Yuro ravine. The ruggedness of the rocky, irregular terrain made it difficult — at times impossible — for the guerrillas to maintain visual contact. Those defending positions at the other entrance to the ravine, some hundreds of meters from Che, among them Inti Peredo, resisted the attack until dark, when they managed to lose the enemy and head toward the previously agreed point of regroupment.

It has been possible to establish that Che continued fighting despite being wounded, until a shot destroyed the barrel of his M-2 rifle, making it totally useless. The pistol he carried had no magazine. These incredible circumstances explain how he could have been captured alive. The wounds in his legs kept him from walking without help, but they were not fatal.

Moved to the town of Higueras, he remained alive some 24 hours. He refused to exchange a single word with his captors, and a drunken officer who tried to annoy him received a slap across the face.

At a meeting in La Paz, Barrientos, Ovando, and other high military leaders coldly made the decision to murder Che. Details are known of the way in which the treacherous agreement was carried out in the school at Higueras. Major Miguel Ayoroa and Colonel Andrés Selnich, rangers trained by the Yankees, ordered warrant officer Mario Terán to proceed with the murder. Terán, completely drunk, entered the school yard. When Che, who heard the shots that had just killed a Bolivian [Simón Cuba (Willy)] and a Peruvian guerrilla fighter [Juan Pablo Chang (Chino)], saw the executioner hesitate, he said firmly, "Shoot! Don't be afraid!" Terán left, and again it was necessary for his superiors, Ayoroa and Selnich, to repeat the order. He then proceeded to carry it out, firing a machine-gun burst from the belt down. A version had already been given out that Che died a few hours after combat; therefore, the executioners had orders not to shoot him in the chest or head, so as not to induce immediately fatal wounds. This cruelly prolonged Che's agony until a sergeant, also drunk, killed him with a pistol shot to the left side. Such a procedure contrasts brutally with the respect shown by Che, without a single exception, toward the lives of the many officers and soldiers of the Bolivian army he took prisoner.

The final hours of his existence in the hands of his contemptible enemies must have been very bitter for him. But no person was better prepared than Che to be put to such a test.

The way in which the diary came into our hands cannot be told at this time; suffice it to say it required no monetary payment. It contains all the notes he wrote from November 7, 1966, the day Che arrived in Ñancahuazú, until October 7, 1967, the evening before the battle in the El Yuro ravine. There are a few pages missing, pages that have not yet arrived in our hands; but they correspond to dates on which nothing of any importance happened, and therefore do not alter the content of the diary in any way.

Although the document itself offers not the slightest doubt as to its authenticity, all photocopies have been subjected to a rigorous examination to establish not only its authenticity but also to check on any possible alteration, no matter how slight. The dates were compared with the diary of one of the surviving guerrilla fighters; both documents coincided in every aspect. Detailed testimony of the other surviving guerrilla fighters, who were witnesses to each one of the events, also contributed to establishing the document's authenticity. In short, it has been established with absolute certainty that all the photostats were faithful copies of Che's diary.

It was a tiring job to decipher the small and difficult hand-writing, a task that was carried out with the tireless assistance of his compañera, Aleida March de Guevara.

The diary will be published almost simultaneously in France by the publishing house of Francois Maspero; in Italy by Feltrinelli publishers; in the Federal Republic of Germany by Trikont Verlag; in the United States by *Ramparts* magazine; in France, in a Spanish edition, by Ediciones Ruedo Ibérico; in Chile by the magazine *Punto Final*; in Mexico by Editorial Siglo XXI; and in other countries.

Hasta la victoria siempre! [Ever onward to victory]

Chapter five

In 1971 Fidel Castro made a visit to Chile, his first trip to another Latin American country in more than a decade. He went at the invitation of then-President Salvador Allende. Allende was overthrown in September 1973 by a U.S.-inspired military coup. The following speech was given in the community of San Miguel in the capital city of Santiago de Chile, which had erected a statue of Che Guevara.

A FEW DAYS AGO, when I visited the statue of José Martí, I said I would come a few days later to visit the statue of Che and meet with the residents of this community.

Today you have honored me with the title "Illustrious Son" of this community, and I thank you for it.

My task here is to give you my impressions and memories, to present some of the characteristics of Che's personality and life.

When I came here and placed flowers in front of the monument, many thoughts went through my mind. First, the memory of one who was a comrade in struggle and a brother of our people and our fighters; the impact of seeing, transformed into bronze, a person I once had the privilege of knowing, at whose side I once had the privilege of fighting.

This is the first time I've seen a monument to someone I've known in life. Usually, when statues are created by artists in memory of people who distinguished themselves for their feats and accomplishments in the struggle for humanity, they symbolize individuals who lived a long time ago, hundreds and even thousands of years ago. Possibly only in very special circumstances does one have the chance to see a statue of someone one has known, because usually history sees fit to erect these monuments after the passage of many years. But in this case the revolutionary proletarian community of San Miguel wanted to erect a monument to Che. And so, in October 1970, three years after his death, this monument was unveiled.

I met Che in Mexico in 1955. An Argentinian by birth, he was Latin American in spirit and in heart. He had just come from Guatemala.

About Che, as about all revolutionaries, many tales have been invented. They try to present him as a conspirator, a shadowy subversive dedicated to devising plots and revolutions. As a young man, like so many other young students, as a graduate of his country's university, like so many other graduates — in his case, as a doctor — Che, who had a special curiosity and interest in things related to Latin America, a special interest in study and knowledge, a special desire to see all our nations, made a tour of several countries. He had nothing more than his degree.

At times on foot, at times on motorcycle, he went from country to country. In fact, when we were in Chuquicamata [in northern Chile] we were shown the place he had stopped for a day on the first trip he made outside his country. He had no money. He wasn't a tourist. He went to see the work centers, the hospitals, the historic sites. He crossed the Andes, took a boat or a raft, and went as far as a leper hospital in the Amazon, where he worked for a time as a doctor.

He continued his journey. He arrived in Guatemala after passing through — if I remember correctly — Brazil, Venezuela, and Colombia. And he arrived in Guatemala when a progressive government headed by Jacobo Arbenz was in power. An agrarian reform was being carried out. Also there at the time were some survivors of the 1953 attack on the Moncada garrison. They established a friendship with Che. He was working there — if I remember correctly — as a doctor.

As one who was interested in the Guatemalan process, a studious man who thirsted after knowledge with an inquiring spirit, a revolutionary vocation and disposition, and a clear intelligence, he had of course read the books and theories of Karl Marx, Engels, and Lenin. And although he wasn't a member of any party, Che was already a Marxist in his thinking.

But it was his lot to live through a bitter experience. While he was in Guatemala the imperialists intervened with an invasion led by the CIA — that is, the CIA organized the invasion of that country from neighboring territory, with arms, planes, and all kinds of equipment. It was something similar to what they later tried to do at Girón [Bay of Pigs]. But in Guatemala, they attacked without any risk. Using their planes and then advancing on the ground, they overthrew the revolutionary government.

The Cubans and other Latin Americans who were there and who had supported the government, who had carried out simple tasks of a practical nature — not even political tasks — had to leave the country. They went to Mexico.

In 1955, the first Moncada combatants who had just come out of prison had to leave Cuba. One of the first comrades subjected to persistent harassment and persecution was Raúl [Castro], who left for Mexico. I arrived a few weeks later. Raúl had already made contact with other comrades who had not been in prison, and he had also met Che. A few days after my arrival in Mexico I met Che in a house where some Cubans were staying on Emparan Street, if I remember the name correctly — but I can't remember the number of the house now.

Che wasn't Che then. He was Ernesto Guevara. It was because of the Argentinian custom of calling people "Che" that the Cubans began calling him Che. That was how he got that name, a name he later made famous, a name he turned into a symbol.

That's how we met. As he himself related in one of his writings, he joined the Cuban movement immediately, after a few hours of discussion.

Because of his state of mind when he left Guatemala, because of the extremely bitter experience he'd lived through there — that cowardly aggression against the country, the interruption of a process that had awakened the hopes of the people — because of his revolutionary vocation, his spirit of struggle, we can't say it took hours, we can say that in a matter of minutes Che decided to join the small group of Cubans who were working on organizing a new phase of the struggle in our country.

We spent a little over a year in Mexico, working under difficult conditions, with very few resources. But that really doesn't matter, that's what was to be expected of the struggle, as with all struggles. Then at last, on November 25, 1956, we left for Cuba.

Our movement had launched a slogan against the skeptics, against those who doubted the possibility of continuing the struggle, against those who disputed our position that in this situation there was no other solution — we had declared that in 1956 we would be either free or martyrs. That declaration was simply a reaffirmation to the Cuban nation of our determination to struggle, of our confidence that the struggle would be renewed without delay.

It is true that many people — not the people in our organization, for they understood perfectly the meaning of that slogan — did not understand why we made that promise to return to Cuba practically on a fixed date. It was because of the state of mind of many people in our country who, because of the frustrations, because of the tricks by the traditional politicians, had become somewhat skeptical. Moreover, there were many people representing vested interests who were engaged in political maneuvering, making great efforts to obtain political agreements with the Batista dictatorship and to extinguish the people's faith in revolutionary struggle.

That was why we were forced to launch that slogan, right or wrong. We aren't going to discuss it now; it may serve as material for theoretical research. People don't always go strictly by a diagram. People don't make history at their own whim or to their own liking. People may contribute to the making of history, but history also makes people. So, for better or worse, the slogan was launched. And for better or worse, we were determined to carry it out.

Special circumstances could and did arise, and there were very serious complications on the eve of our departure. But we had always had a small number of arms hidden, and we said that if we can't all go, some of us will, no matter what. So 82 fighters left aboard a small cabin cruiser called *Granma*. We sailed 2,400 kilometers and arrived at the coast of Cuba on December 2, 1956. Two or three days from now our country will be celebrating the 15th anniversary of that landing, which marked the birth of our small army. December 2 is now our Armed Forces Day.

That's the way the struggle began. I don't propose to give you an entire history — far from it. I simply want to provide you with a clear understanding of the circumstances in which this contingent began the struggle.

And what was Che? Che was the doctor of our contingent. He wasn't the commissar. He didn't yet have any troops under his command. He was simply the doctor.

Because of his seriousness, his intelligence, and his character, Che had once been assigned leader of a group of Cubans in a house in Mexico. One day a small, disagreeable incident took place. There were about 20 or 30 Cubans there in all, and some of them — it must have been two or three, but sometimes two or three are enough to create a disagreeable situation — challenged Che's leadership because he was an Argentinian and not a Cuban.

We of course criticized an attitude that ignored human value; that ingratitude toward someone who, although not born in our land, was ready to shed his blood for it. And I remember the incident hurt me a great deal. I think it hurt him as well.

He was, in addition, a person without any desire to exercise authority. He did not have the slightest ambition, he was not self-centered in any way. He was instead a person who became inhibited if anyone contradicted him.

When he came to our country, he came — I repeat — as our troop doctor, on the General Staff. The interesting thing is how Che became a soldier, how he distinguished himself, and what his characteristics were.

A few examples: on December 5, because of tactical errors, our small detachment was the victim of a surprise attack and was completely dispersed. After overcoming tremendous difficulties, a small number of men regrouped in the midst of an encirclement and heavy pursuit. There were three groups: one with Raúl, another group that included Che, who wasn't yet in charge of a group — comrade Almeida was in this group too — and the group with me. Almeida's group rejoined mine first, and Raúl's did so a few days later. We continued the struggle.

Our first battle took place January 17, 1957; we had 17 men. At the beginning, of all the weapons we had brought with us, we were able to round up only seven. December 5 was what we might call the baptism by fire for Che and many other comrades. But the first small battle we won was on January 17.

By the second battle Che had already begun to distinguish himself, to show he was Che. In a confrontation with forces that were pursuing us, he showed his personal bravery. In a practically individual battle with an enemy soldier, in the midst of general combat, he shot the adversary and crawled forward under a hail of bullets to take his weapon. He carried out that brave, outstanding, and special deed on his own initiative, and it earned him the admiration of all.

Barely six or seven days later, at the end of January, we suffered the consequences of a betrayal. Our small contingent had grown to some 30 men, five or six of whom were peasants who had asked for and received permission to go visit their families — discipline still wasn't very strong in that small group. They left their weapons there, with the detachment. One day at dawn, a squadron of fighter planes and bombers attacked with a very heavy barrage at the exact spot where the detachment was located — at least that's how we viewed it at the time. We had already had some experience along that line, but this was the hardest we had ever been hit.

I'm going into this because when the combatants were trying to get away from the spot where the fire was concentrated — we were going up a hillside — at that moment we remembered the weapons that belonged to the five or six peasants who were visiting their homes. Those weapons had to be retrieved and I called for volunteers. Immediately, without thinking or hesitating for an instant, Che was the first to say, "I'll go." He and another comrade went quickly to the place being bombed, got the weapons, hid them in a safe place, and then rejoined the rest of our forces.

Different episodes took place. Che was still the doctor; he didn't command any troops. But in May of that year, on May 28, something else happened. Our column already had some 100 men, if I remember correctly, and a group of Cuban revolutionaries from another political organization had landed in the northern part of the province. We remembered our own landing and the difficult moments we had gone through; we wanted to help that group by carrying out a support action. So we started for the coast, where an enemy infantry company held positions with fortifications and trenches.

Basing ourselves on the information we had received, we scheduled the attack for dawn and organized it very quickly. But when we were about to start combat at dawn the situation became complicated; it turned out our information was not very accurate. The enemy positions were not where we thought they were, and the situation became complicated. However, we had to go ahead.

Our small units — platoons and squads — were scattered in a circle whose perimeter was at least a kilometer and a half long. We could not retreat. We had no choice but to attack.

At the time of that battle, Che was a part of the General Staff. He already had some responsibilities. We had to carry out two or three actions. We had to ask Almeida's platoon to advance to the front quickly to get as close as possible to certain enemy positions. The advance was very risky and cost us a number of casualties.

We also had to have a group move toward the west. And while we were sizing up the situation and analyzing the necessity of that action, Che immediately volunteered. He asked for a group of men and an automatic rifle, and said he would march to the west. We gave him a group of men and the automatic rifle, which virtually belonged to the General Staff, and he quickly began the advance toward that position.

That was the third time that when we needed a volunteer, Che had immediately stepped forward. In any difficult situation he would act at once, and that's what he did then.

That battle was a hard fought one. It lasted three hours and almost 30 percent of the forces on both sides were killed or wounded. It had been motivated by the desire to help those who had landed in the north. Despite our efforts, however, they had been surrounded, captured, and killed — every last one of them. When we occupied the enemy camp, after three hours of fighting, there was a large number of wounded — enemy wounded and our own men. Che was the doctor who attended quickly to both our wounded and those of the enemy. That was always the practice and the rule throughout our struggle.

Later, logically, the battle gave rise to a concentration of enemy forces, a huge manhunt directed against us. And we had to solve the problem of our many wounded. After we took care of the enemy wounded — we left them there at the scene of the battle so that, as we withdrew, they could be picked up by their own side — Che as the doctor stayed behind in an isolated place with our wounded. He took care of them in a difficult situation in which sizable enemy forces in the area were trying to corner us.

The column marched through difficult, rugged terrain. We broke through the encirclement. But Che stayed behind with the wounded, with only a very few men. He stayed with them for several weeks until the wounded had recovered. The small group was then able to rejoin the main column, which had been reinforced by the weapons we had captured during the battle.

So the first time we organized a new column — the second column — we gave command of that column to Che. And we made him commander, the second commander of our forces. With his small new column, he began to operate in a specific area, in positions not far from where the first column was based.

That was how Che became a soldier and was named commander of a small column. And, of course, he continued to display the same character, the same attitude, to such an extent that it can be said we had to watch out for him.

What do I mean by watching out for him? Well, his aggressiveness and audacity led him to plan very daring operations. And when he entered combat during the following stage, which lasted several months — a stage where his small group still lacked sufficient forces and experience in the region they were operating in — he displayed great tenacity and perseverance as a soldier. Sometimes he insisted on fighting with the enemy for a position. And there he would stay and fight for hours, even days.

We could say that, in a way, he even violated the rules — that is, the ideal norms, the most perfect methods — of combat, risking his life in battle because of that character, tenacity, and spirit of his. He would obstinately refuse to surrender a position even though his little column was very small and the advancing enemy forces very numerous, even when there wasn't much sense in defending that particular position. That was his character; that was his perseverance; that was his combative spirit.

Logically, therefore, we had to lay down certain rules and guidelines for him to follow.

What was it that we admired in him, that impressed us? What was that characteristic that gave the precise measure of Che's spirit and soul? It was his moral qualities, his altruism, his absolute selflessness. He had met a group of Cubans; he became convinced of their cause; and from the very first moment he showed great selflessness and generosity. From the first moment, he was absolutely willing to give his life, regardless of whether it was in the first battle or the second or the third. Here we had a person born in a place thousands of kilometers from our country, a person some Cubans had even once objected to because he was giving them orders and hadn't been born in Cuba, but for that country and for that cause, he was the first at every moment to volunteer for something dangerous, for a mission with great risks.

He was someone who had no personal ambitions whatsoever. There was nothing he wanted except to do his duty and to do it well. He sought to respond quickly in any situation, to immediately and unhesitatingly set an example of what he thought a revolutionary fighter should be.

During those early days, how far Che was from imagining that one day, in this community, there would be a meeting such as this and we would be standing in front of a monument honoring him!

Che did not fight for glory, for material possessions, or ambition. He never fought for fame. He was a person who right from the outset, from the very first battle, was ready to give his life; who could have been killed as just one more soldier. If he had died in the first battle, he would have left behind the memory of his person, the personality and characteristics we knew him by, and nothing more. The same if he had died in the second, third, fourth, or fifth battle. He could have died in any of those battles; many did.

Therefore, we can say that Che thought of nothing but duty and sacrifice, with the most absolute purity and with the most complete selflessness.

We can say that Che survived the battles in the Sierra Maestra because we followed the principle that whenever a person distinguished themselves as a leader, we would not expose them in minor battles but would save them for more important operations.

An offensive was launched against us in May 1958, when some 10,000 [soldiers of the Batista dictatorship] advanced against our forces — at the time we had at most 300 soldiers, including Che's column and some other forces we had managed to get together. After a battle that lasted 70 consecutive days, our soldiers, who were already combat-tested veterans — in spite of being at a disadvantage with regard to weapons and numbers — managed to smash the offensive, capture a sizable number of weapons, and organize different columns. When the battle began, we had 300 men; when it ended we had 805 armed men.

It was then that we organized two columns — one commanded by Camilo and the other by Che — equipped with the best weapons we had, and they carried out what we can call a veritable feat. Starting from the Sierra Maestra — Camilo with 90 men, Che with 140 — they marched toward the west, toward Las Villas Province, across more than 500 kilometers of flatlands, uninhabited in many places. The two columns left the Sierra Maestra around September. They advanced with the enemy close on their heels, many times fighting their way over difficult terrain, and carried out their mission of reaching the center of the island.

When, at the end of December, our forces were virtually in control of Oriente Province, and the island was cut in two through Las Villas Province, Che performed one of his last military feats in Cuba. He marched on the city of Santa Clara with 300 combatants, attacked an armored train stationed on the outskirts of the city, cut the tracks between the train and the main headquarters of the enemy, derailed the train, surrounded it, forced the troops inside to surrender, and captured all the weapons there. In short, he attacked the city of Santa Clara with only 300 men.

When the Batista regime finally collapsed on January 1 and

there was an attempt to cheat the Cuban revolution of its triumph, the columns of Camilo and Che were ordered to advance rapidly on Havana. They carried out their mission; on January 2 both columns were inside the capital of the republic. Victory was consolidated on that day, and a long road began.

Everybody's life changed. Many tasks arose and many combatants had to take on administrative responsibilities. At the end of several months, Che was named minister of industry and began to carry out the work that occupied him for several years.

I have spoken of Che as a soldier but he was endowed with outstanding qualities in many areas. First of all, he was a person of extraordinary culture; he had one of the most penetrating minds I have known, one of the most generous spirits, one of the most revolutionary characters. His feelings — his concern for other people, his concern for the movement in Asia and Africa — extended to the whole world.

At the time the Algerians were fighting for their independence [from France, in a war from 1954 to 1962]. The poor and underdeveloped countries in other continents were also engaged in different struggles. He saw with complete clarity the need to establish contact with these worlds. He visited many countries on different missions, seeking closer relations and commercial trade, working hard to overcome the consequences of the economic blockade imposed on our country.

When the Playa Girón [Bay of Pigs] invasion took place, Che was in command of the forces of Pinar del Río Province. When the attack against Playa Girón began, in the south-central part of the island, we didn't know at first where the direction of the main attack would be. Generally speaking, the most experienced leaders assumed command of specific military zones. And even though he was in charge of the Ministry of Industry, as soon as the mobilization against the attack began, Che was sent to Pinar del Río Province. Similarly, when the October [Missile] Crisis occurred, in 1962 — another moment of very grave danger — Che again assumed command of that military region.

Thus, a number of times and under different circumstances, we were obliged to confront certain grave dangers. And he continued to serve as a combatant, he assumed his responsibilities, he continued studying military science assiduously.

He was an extremely studious person who, in the hours in which he could manage to free himself from his intense work, sacrificed sleep and rest to study. Not only did he work interminable hours in the Ministry of Industry, but he also received visitors, wrote accounts of the war and about his experiences in the countries he visited on one or another mission. He related his experiences in an interesting, simple, and clear style.

Many episodes of the revolutionary war have been preserved because Che wrote them down, because of his interest in making available for our people the experiences written down by their compatriots at various times.

Che was the originator of voluntary work in Cuba. He was a person who maintained close contact with the workplaces that were under the responsibility of the Ministry of Industry. He visited them, talked with the workers, analyzed the problems. Every Sunday Che went to some workplace; sometimes to the docks to load freight with the dock workers; sometimes to the mines to work with the miners; sometimes to the cane fields to cut cane; sometimes he met with construction workers. He never kept a Sunday for himself.

What's more, all this and his previous feats must be viewed in the light of his own health, for he suffered from certain allergy problems that produced severe attacks of asthma. With asthma, he fought during the whole campaign. With asthma, he worked day and night. With asthma, he wrote. With asthma, he traveled throughout the country and the world. With asthma, he went down into the mines, went to work in the fields, went everywhere without ever allowing himself a moment's rest. When he wasn't working at his responsibilities in the ministry, he was studying during hours stolen from sleep, or he was out doing voluntary work.

Che was a person with infinite confidence and faith in humanity. He was a living example. It was his style to be the example, to set the example. He was a person with a great spirit of self-sacrifice, with a truly spartan nature, capable of any kind of self-denial. His policy was to set the example.

We could say that his entire life was an example in every sphere. He was a person of absolute moral integrity, of unshakably firm principles, a complete revolutionary who looked toward the future, toward the humanity of the future, and who above all stressed human values, humanity's moral values. And above all, he practiced selflessness, renunciation, self-denial.

None of the words I use about him involve the slightest exaggeration, the slightest overestimation. They simply describe the man we knew.

Here is his monument, here is his figure as the artist saw it. But it is impossible for a monument to capture the overall conception of the person. We have Che's writings, his narratives, his speeches. Those who knew him have their own memory of Che. And we have seen how proudly the workers in many of our factories recall the day Che visited their workplaces, the places where Che did voluntary work.

Not very long ago, we visited a large textile plant whose machinery was being upgraded. We were accompanied by an illustrious foreign visitor. The workers there took us to a shop where they kept, almost like a family treasure, the looms on which Che had done voluntary work. The mines Che visited and the places where he worked and talked with the workers are other monuments to his memory, which our workers cherish with extraordinary affection.

But Che did not live for history; he did not live for honors or glory. Like every other true revolutionary, like every other thoroughgoing revolutionary, he knew what that extraordinary person, that great patriot José Martí — whom you have also honored here — meant when he said, "All the glory of the world fits into a kernel of corn."

Revolutionaries do not struggle for honor or glory, or to occupy a place in history. Che occupied, occupies, and will always occupy a great place in history because that was not important to him, because he was ready to die from the first battle on, because he was always absolutely selfless. And so his life became an epic, his life became an example. We say to our people — and this has become a basic idea, a watchword — if we were to describe what we want our children to be like, we would want them to be like Che. There is no Cuban family, no Cuban parent, no Cuban child who doesn't hold Che up as the model for their life.

If today's world — this contemporary world that is writing a new history of humanity, that is trying to build a better, more humane society, that confronts very complex problems and difficult struggles — if today's world is seeking an example, and if you consider the qualities this example requires, we who knew Che, we who had that great privilege, understand why our people and our country have chosen this model for our children. And we believe it is an extraordinarily worthy one.

How wonderful it would be if we were to succeed in making this model a reality in the generations to come so that in the future we would have generations like Che!

Future societies will be made of generations of people like Che! From generations of people like Che a better society, communism, will arise!

He left us his example. And as the final fruit of his clear mind, his spartan character, his heart of steel — steel for self-sacrifice, for suffering — of his noble, sensitive, and generous spirit of giving himself to a cause and struggling for others, sacrificing himself for others, of his intelligence, his heart, and his calm hand, he left us, finally, his diary, in which he narrated the epic of the last days of his life. And in his concise, straight-forward, terse style, reflecting the last moments of his life, he wrote a true epic of literature, containing extraordinary merit in every sense.

That is why the youth of the world see Che as a symbol. And just as he identified with the cause of the Algerians, the Vietnamese, and the Latin Americans, so Che's name and figure are viewed with tremendous respect, admiration, and affection on all continents. The name and figure of Che are emblazoned even there in the very heart of U.S. society itself. Civil rights fighters, fighters against the war of aggression, fighters for peace, progressives, all citizens who struggle for any cause whatever within the United States itself, have taken up Che's name and banner. He has therefore become a gigantic figure, and so he is. But nobody's imagination, nobody's fantasy, nobody's self-interest created this. Never has a banner been raised on a more solid pedestal, never has an example been raised on firmer ground.

Che himself turned his figure into this symbol during his brief but intense life, his brief but creative life. This was not his aim; this was not what he sought. But because of his life, his selflessness, his nobility, his altruism, his heroism, he became what he is today. He became a banner, a model, a fighter. He became a guide. He became a monument to all that is noble, to the spirit of justice. Che is, in short, a model as a revolutionary, as a fighter, and as a communist for all the peoples of the world.

Chapter six

The following is part of a 1987 interview with Fidel Castro by Italian journalist Gianni Minà at the time of the 20th anniversary of Che's death. The entire interview was published as An encounter with Fidel.

Gianni Minà: President Castro, you are a witness to contemporary history like few others in our time. This interview is proof of that. I would like to move on to your most intimate recollections of some comrades in struggle, in particular Che Guevara and Camilo Cienfuegos. For example, Che represents a symbol, an ideal, for at least three generations in Europe and the world. When you think of your friend Che, what is the first thought that comes to your mind?

Fidel Castro: For me, as well, it has been hard to accept the thought that Che is dead. I have dreamed many times — you sometimes tell people the things you dream — I dreamed I spoke with him, that he was alive. It's a very special thing, a person whose death it is hard to resign yourself to. What's the reason? In my opinion, it is because he has a permanent presence in everything.

His death occurred far away, many kilometers from our country. The idea that Che was dead was something very difficult to get used to. It hit me differently from the death of other comrades, for we have lost comrades in the struggle many times. We have seen comrades die. One has the impression Che is still present because of what he symbolizes, because of his character, his conduct, his principles. He had a great number of truly exceptional qualities. I knew him very well, from the time he made contact with us in Mexico until he left Cuba the final time.

I really think, with sorrow, that with Che's death a great mind was lost. He was a person who still had much to contribute to the theory and practice of building socialism.

Gianni Minà: In the letter to you that Che wrote before leaving he seems almost bitter for not having earlier recognized your quality as a leader, for the time it took him to fully recognize that.
Fidel Castro: What might be the reason for that? First, Che was a very quiet man. He was not expressive. He didn't communicate these things. He felt things but he did not say them. By the way, some very warm-hearted verses he wrote about me have come to light; someone saved them.

He was naturally a little skeptical about Latin America, about Latin American politicians. He may have thought our revolution might end the way other revolutions have ended. But in reality he never gave me the slightest impression of having such doubts. He was always extraordinarily fraternal and respectful with me. He may have been a little mistrustful of the [July 26] Movement. He may have observed that our Movement was heterogeneous, that it included people from many different sectors.

He already had an excellent revolutionary education, a Marxist education. He was very studious. He had graduated from medical school, conducted research, and was very rigorous in studying the questions of Marxism. So for this reason he was a little skeptical. I think if he wrote that it must have been from an excess of integrity. Because in reality I had to coordinate many factors and to promote unity over the reservations demonstrated by one or another comrade; I had to have patience in my relations with them.

For Che, who was impulsive, very courageous, very daring, at times even reckless, I always had special regard. On more than one occasion he would step forward as a volunteer. Whatever the mission, the first volunteer was always Che. He volunteered for the most difficult actions and suggested them in the midst of combat. He was totally selfless and altruistic. Cuba wasn't his homeland, yet he had joined us and every day he was ready to give his life for the revolution.

I would, of course, use cadres according to the importance of a mission. When a cadre had acquired more skills, more experience, we would send out new cadres so they too could learn and develop. In war you can't continually use a cadre in dangerous situations, because at one moment or another you will lose them. We really had to protect the cadres, preserve them, because they wanted to do things. And I took on the task of preserving them as much as possible and using them in the most important missions.

I often rotated the men in this type of task, but as for him... Well, I truly believe if we hadn't followed this policy, Che — because of those character traits of his — would not have come out of the war alive. But Che was exceedingly straightforward. If at any moment he thought there was some doubt about something, he felt obligated to speak up about it. That's the way he was.

Gianni Minà: The Cuban revolution is incredible. It united an intellectual like Che, an intellectual like you, and a simple man of the people like Camilo — men of different backgrounds and educational levels, who functioned together in harmony. There was clearly a common dream.

Fidel Castro: They were three people of three different origins, different characteristics.

What is extraordinary about Che is that he wasn't Cuban, he was Argentinian. When we met in Mexico, he had been working in Guatemala as a doctor. He was filled with enthusiasm by the political process in Guatemala, by the agrarian reform. He witnessed the intervention of the United States and suffered very much over all that. It was something he carried within him. He joined us right away. As he relates, he joined us the first time we had a conversation.

He envisioned an anti-imperialist revolution, a revolution of national liberation. He did not yet see the socialist revolution — he envisioned that to be a little bit down the road — but he committed himself totally.

Moreover, Che was our doctor. No one thought of Che as being a great soldier. He liked sports. He tried to climb Popocatépetl almost every week; he never reached the top, but tried every week. He suffered from asthma; he had that handicap, but he made a heroic effort to climb that volcano. Although he never made it to the top, he never stopped trying to climb it once more. That also shows what kind of character he had. He was our doctor, he went as our doctor because he had that handicap. No one imagined him as a soldier. But he wasn't only an intellectual; he was also to become a great soldier.

Camilo was a man of the people. At first no one could have guessed his qualities. Later he really distinguished himself. I am sure many more would have done so, because in our group of 82 men — I later gave this quite a bit of thought — there were some 40 who were suited to become leaders. Out of those few who survived, several brilliant leaders emerged: Camilo, Che, and other comrades, including one outstanding leader not mentioned so much — Raúl.

Gianni Minà: How were Camilo and Che different?
Fidel Castro: They had two different personalities, even though they loved and respected each other very much. Camilo liked to joke a lot, he always had a sense of humor.

Gianni Minà: Cuban.
Fidel Castro: He had a Cuban sense of humor, always laughing, very daring, very intelligent, less intellectual than Che but also an excellent leader, one who never gave the enemy an opportunity. He was very courageous, but wasn't as reckless as Che. Che seemed to be a man who sought death. Camilo defied death; he wasn't afraid of it, but he wasn't reckless. Those are two differences between them. They had great affection for each other.

Gianni Minà: And your brother, Raúl?
Fidel Castro: Another leader who, as I said, is not mentioned so much in this connection. Raúl is capable, responsible, and brilliant. He also played a very important role.

Of the group that survived, several very good leaders emerged. That's why I think there were many young men who, had they survived the initial expedition, were well suited to become leaders. At least 15 or 20 outstanding leaders could have emerged from our group — because someone needs both the opportunity and responsibilities to distinguish themselves.

Gianni Minà: More than 20 years ago Che left Cuba to fight in Bolivia. Can you tell me where he went from the time he left Havana until he arrived in Bolivia?

Fidel Castro: Che very much wanted to go to South America. This was an old idea of his, because when he joined us in Mexico — although it is not that he made it a condition — he did ask one thing: "The only thing I want after the victory of the revolution is to go fight in Argentina" — his country — "that you don't keep me from doing so, that no reasons of state will stand in the way." And I promised him that. It was a long way off, after all. Firstly, no one knew if we would win the war or who was going to be alive at the end — and he surely, because of his impetuousness, had little chance of coming out alive — but this is what he asked. Once in a while, in the Sierra and afterward, he would remind me of this plan and promise. He was certainly farsighted in this.

After gaining experience in the Sierra Maestra, he grew more enthusiastic about the idea of making a revolution in South America, in his own country. Che knew firsthand our exceptional experience, beginning with the difficult conditions in which we rebuilt our army and carried through the struggle, and he developed a great faith in the possibilities of the revolutionary movement in South America. When I speak of South America, I am actually speaking of the southern part of South America. The promise had been given and I always told him, "Don't worry, we will keep our word." He raised it perhaps two or three times.

With the triumph of the revolution there were many tasks to carry out and problems of all kinds to be resolved. We had political problems, problems with the unification of our forces, state problems, economic problems, all such things. Now no one knew what a great soldier Che would turn out to be. He was, as I said, our doctor, who began to distinguish himself in the first battles and was to become a great military leader. Both he and Camilo carried out a very important task in the war — the invasion of the central part of the country, under difficult conditions. Much more could be said about that, but this is not the time.

We had to confront all the tasks of a victorious revolution, where nothing remained of the former state, the old armed forces, or the administrative apparatus. The various revolutionary organizations — although ours carried the principal weight — had the support of the immense majority of the population, and we used our influence to bring about unity. We always fought sectarianism. We experienced a process of unity of the revolutionary forces. Camilo took part in all this but his death was very premature; it occurred in October [1959] in connection with the events in Camagüey and the problem of Huber Matos.

Che was later assigned to head the Ministry of Industry. He worked very methodically. He also had several other responsibilities. Every time a serious comrade was needed for an important post, Che would offer to do it. He was named president of the National Bank in the days when technicians, specialists in banking but politically inconsistent, were abandoning the country. Jokes and anecdotes followed. People would say that we had asked for an economist and Che volunteered. And we asked him, "You're an economist?" "No," he answered, "I'm a communist." The struggle inside the country was just beginning, and right-wing elements were accusing Che of being a communist and all kinds of things such as that.

But Che always had great authority. Every assignment he was given he would fulfill strictly and brilliantly. He worked hard and acquired his first experiences in building socialism in the sector of nationalized industry. He worked hard in organizing production, in checking production, in voluntary work. He was one of the pioneers of voluntary work. He participated in almost every activity. He was very consistent in everything he did; he set an example in everything he did.

That is how he spent the first years of the revolution. He later evidently began to feel impatient about carrying out his old plans and ideas. I believe he was influenced in part by the fact that time was passing. He knew that special physical conditions were required for this. He felt he was capable of doing it and, in reality, he was at the peak of his mental and physical capacities. He had many ideas, based on the experience he had gained in Cuba, of what could be done in his native country. He was primarily thinking of his country, but didn't think only of Argentina. He thought of all the Americas, of South America in general.

He was impatient. From our own experience, I knew the difficulty of the initial phase of a process like the one he wanted to carry out. I thought better conditions could be created for what he was thinking of doing. We attempted to persuade him not to be impatient, to convince him that more time was needed. He wanted to go out from the very first day and do it all, while we wanted other, less well-known cadres to carry out the initial steps.

Che was also very interested in international questions, in the problems faced by Africa. At the time, mercenaries had intervened in the former Belgian Congo, now Zaire. Lumumba had been killed, a neocolonial regime was established, and a movement of armed struggle emerged in Zaire. We never made this public, but the revolutionary movement asked us for help and we sent instructors and combatants on an internationalist mission.

Gianni Minà: And the movement of Lumumba?
Fidel Castro: At that time Soumialot was its leader. It was the same movement, but Lumumba was dead.

I myself suggested an idea to Che. He had time on his hands, he had to wait. At the same time he wanted to train cadres, to develop their experience. So we put him in charge of the group that was going to help the revolutionaries in what is today Zaire. They went in by way of Tanzania, crossing Lake Tanganyika. In all, about 100 Cubans went and stayed there several months.

He followed the approach of teaching Zairians how to fight. Cubans and Zairian patriots fought white mercenaries and forces sent by the government. They fought many battles against the mercenaries. The idea was not to fight the war in place of the Zairians but rather to help them, to teach them how to fight.

But that movement was just beginning. It didn't have sufficient strength or unity. In the end the revolutionary leaders of the former Belgian colony decided to halt the struggle, and our personnel were withdrawn. That decision was quite correct. It had become clear that conditions did not exist at the time for developing the struggle. The Zairians analyzed the situation along with the Cuban contingent, and we were in agreement with their assessment. Consequently the unit was withdrawn, and the Cuban personnel returned home.

Having now spent about six months in Zaire, Che stayed for a while in Tanzania, assessing the experience he had just lived through. His conduct on the mission was, as always, exemplary to the highest degree. His stay in Africa was temporary, awaiting the creation of conditions for traveling to South America.

During this whole period the situation became highly awkward for us, as Che had already said goodbye. He had written the letter before he left, and he left quietly of course — you might even say clandestinely. We kept the letter quiet and this gave rise to many rumors as well as some genuine slanders. Some said that Che had been made to disappear, others that Che was dead, or that there were differences — all sorts of stories. We took that downpour of rumors and intrigues silently, so as not to endanger the mission he wanted to accomplish and the personnel he intended to take to his final destination — South America.

So after finishing the phase in Zaire he went to Tanzania, marking time. He spent some months in Tanzania and then went to a socialist country in Eastern Europe. In fact... Well, I'm not going to say more, because I haven't checked with the country in question to see if it can be told. He stayed there. He didn't want to return to Cuba because it would have been an embarrassment to come back after the publication of the letter.

Eventually, publication of the letter became unavoidable. It was becoming very harmful to allow the campaign of slander to continue without an answer, an explanation to world public opinion. The only alternative was to publish the letter. The letter, of course, said nothing specific about his mission. He spoke only of fighting in other parts of the world.

Once the letter had been made public — politically, it had become unavoidable to publish it — Che, with his particular character, felt very awkward about returning to Cuba after having said farewell. But in the end I persuaded him to return, because it was the best move given all the practical matters he wanted to take care of. So he secretly returned to Cuba. He stayed several months, training in a remote mountainous region. He spent months in training with those who were to accompany him.

He asked for the collaboration of a group of comrades — some were veteran guerrilla fighters, some were new men who had been in Zaire with him. He asked for their help. He selected the group and spoke with each one of them. We authorized the selection of a group of highly experienced comrades to accompany him, because the task he intended to carry out really required a group of experienced volunteers. He trained with them for several months while groundwork was undertaken to arrange for transporting him and his group to Bolivia.

Che chose the territory and worked out the plan of struggle. We gave him cooperation and support in carrying out the project, although naturally we were concerned about the inherent risks. We would have preferred a movement that was already much more developed, a movement Che could join; but he wanted to get there almost at the very beginning. We managed to hold him until at least some preliminary work had been carried out, so he could go there with a little more safety. The initial stages are the most difficult.

In fact, all this was organized perfectly, down to the last detail. Che and the other comrades were transported to a camp in the area selected. They had to overcome difficult obstacles, pass through complicated places. It wasn't easy, but it was accomplished thanks to the methods used. They managed to join with a group of comrades in the area of Ñancahuazú, I believe it's called, in the part of Bolivia he chose.

That was more or less the itinerary: a stay in Africa, leaving via Tanzania; eastern Zaire; a return to Tanzania; a socialist country in Europe; Cuba again and, finally, the trip to the area he had selected in Bolivia.

Gianni Minà: Was it a mistake to have chosen Bolivia, where the people were probably not yet ready for a revolution? Was it a romantic error determined by a geographic choice that was neither tactically nor strategically justified?
Fidel Castro: I wouldn't say that. He was interested in Argentina,

he was genuinely inspired by the idea of making a revolution in Argentina. But at that time we had no relations with any country in South America — all those governments had joined with the United States against Cuba. In the early days Che had recruited a group of Argentinians, including Jorge Ricardo Massetti, who worked with us in the Sierra Maestra as a journalist and who later founded Prensa Latina. Che had recruited him to his ideas of struggle in Argentina. Massetti, in agreement with Che, attempted to establish a front in northern Argentina, in the Salta area. Massetti died on that mission.

Che was always a very sensitive man, highly committed to his comrades. The mere fact that he had initiated the effort, the struggle, in which some comrades had already given their lives was without doubt a factor that greatly influenced his impatience to carry out his plans. He had already studied the area in question. And the importance of the area he selected seems to have been its proximity to the Argentinian border.

Che knew the Bolivian peasants were very quiet, reserved, and mistrustful. He knew they were very different from Cuban peasants. After graduating from medical school, he had traveled through South America on a motorbike. He visited a number of places, even as far as the Amazon. He had extensive contact with the people there and knew the tragedy of the Indians, their characteristics. He knew this very well and felt it deeply. More than once he explained to me, told me what they were like, how you had to work with them, how this took time, that it wasn't easy. He was conscious of the difficulties of the task ahead.

So what happened? He had witnessed our experience, our almost incredible experience. After the initial setbacks, he saw how a very small group could reorganize and carry out a struggle under very difficult conditions. He had blind faith in this type of struggle and its possibilities, even more so now that he had enormous experience in it.

So Che chose the territory, the place. And essentially, I would say he made no mistake in his choice. No mistake was made. He tried to gain the support of organized political forces. He assumed he could count on the support of the Bolivian Communist Party and other forces. It turned out that other forces joined him, because there were divisions at that time within the left, within the communist movement.

Gianni Minà: In this regard, Che's father has said publicly that the Bolivian Communist Party is responsible for Che's death: that if they did not betray him, they surely left him to die. And is it true, as Régis Debray has said, that Che could have been saved if an expedition of young Bolivian Communists had set out from Cochabamba?

Fidel Castro: I share none of these views. And I believe I am very well informed on these questions.

The Communist Party had various leaders. The general secretary, Mario Monje, had already been spoken with, and an agreement of sorts had been reached. But other leaders were involved as well. It was that, really, that led to the conflict with Monje. That is well known, it's part of history. A conflict arose between Che and Monje over certain of Monje's positions, perhaps over pretensions of his concerning leadership, pretensions Che did not accept.

I believe that formal factors prevailed in Monje's thinking, along the lines that it was his country where action was to begin, that he was the general secretary of the party. But in reality there was no one, no cadre, better prepared than Che to lead an action that transcended the borders of Bolivia. This gave rise to misunderstandings, and they were not able to reach agreement. Monje withdrew his support.

We received this information and immediately arranged meetings here with other important and prestigious leaders of the party, with Kolle and with Simón Reyes, a well-known and very good workers' leader. I asked them to come to Cuba, spoke with them, and told them: "A crisis has emerged, and it's a very delicate situation. I have asked you to come meet with us because it is essential that you give Che some help."

They promised to help, they were ready to provide assistance and collaboration. They did everything possible, although in disagreement with the party secretary. What happened is that the pace of events quickened, and there was no chance for them to help. But they had an excellent attitude and understood

(Photo: Osvaldo Salas)

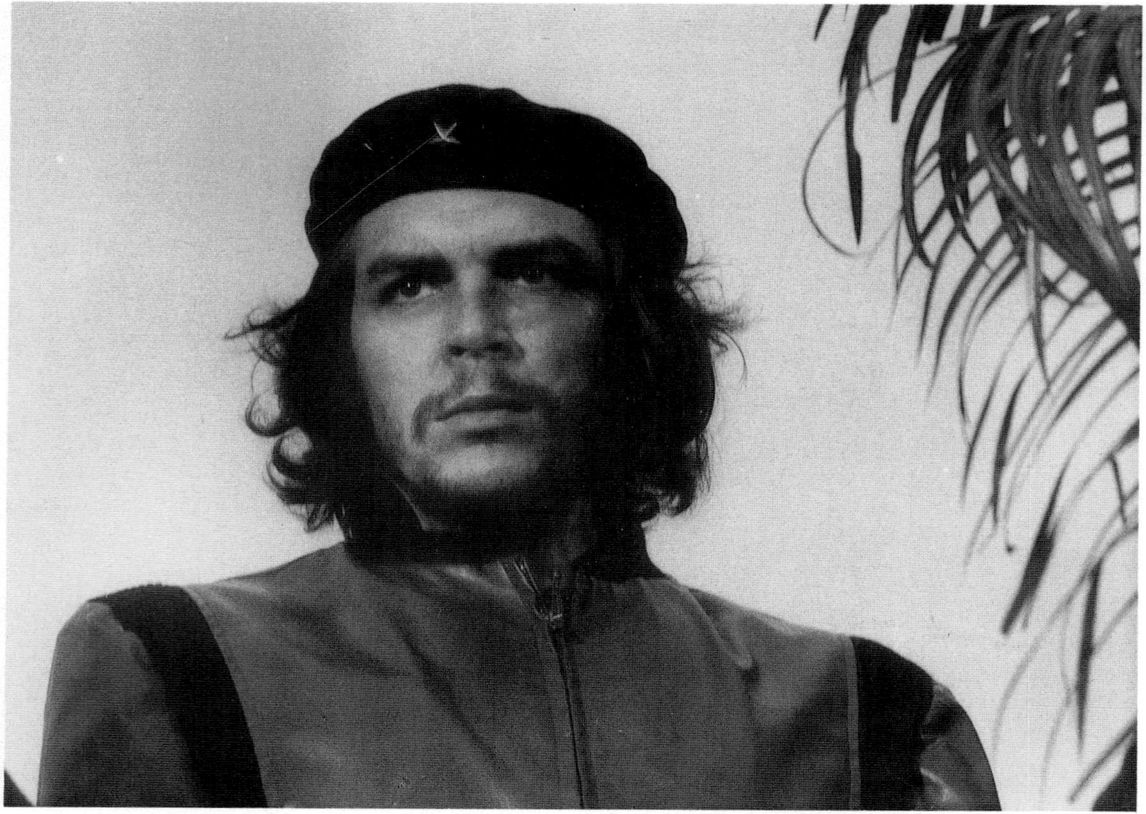

Photo: Korda

Che Guevara in Africa, 1965

Che Guevara in disguise before leaving Cuba in 1966 for Bolivia

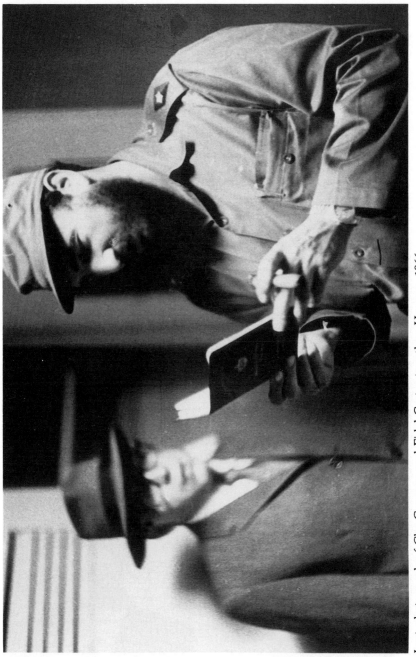

Last photograph of Che Guevara and Fidel Castro together, Havana, 1966

Photos distributed by the United States through the Organization of
American States showing Che Guevara in Bolivia in 1967. The bottom
photo shows the passport used by Guevara to enter Bolivia.

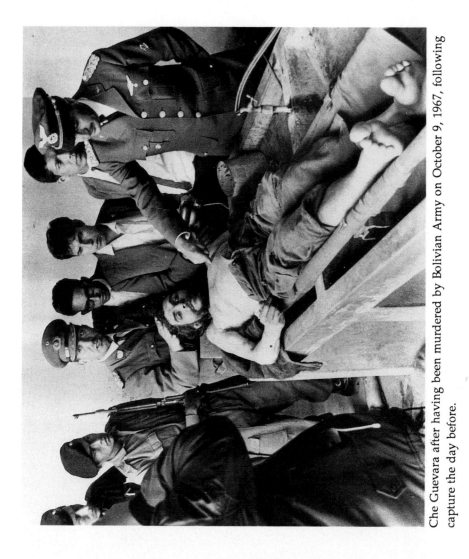

Che Guevara after having been murdered by Bolivian Army on October 9, 1967, following capture the day before.

Image of Che Guevara behind presidium, October 18, 1967
(Photo: Osvaldo Salas)

everything in the meeting I had with them. Kolle later became leader of the party, replacing Monje. Simón Reyes also took on important responsibilities in the party leadership. They were part of the Communist Party and they made a commitment.

When we received information about this sort of situation, that is the kind of solution we sought. We managed to gain the support of other movements and also of a few Latin Americans. This was the stage the work was at when events became complicated and, in fact, their presence was discovered. For one reason or another, a combination of factors, the detachment was spotted while it was still in the stage of organization. I believe they needed a little bit more time.

Monje bears a certain responsibility, but historically it would be unjust to blame the Communist Party as a whole. A number of Communists joined Che. These included the Peredo brothers, excellent people who proved to be very fine cadres. They joined and supported Che, gave him a great deal of help. And important cadres in the party leadership differed with Monje and wanted to help Che. So when responsibility is assigned, it should be given to Monje; but you cannot accuse the entire Communist Party or blame it for the way events developed.

Gianni Minà: In Europe it is also said...
Fidel Castro: As for Debray, I didn't even respond to that because it belongs to the realm of fantasy. Yes, it is only fantasy, because not even the most minimal conditions existed to organize a column that could have helped Che. There were no weapons, no trained combatants, and no trainees. It's a theory, it can only be spoken of as a theory; it's a fantasy. You have to understand this is not regular war, it's guerrilla war, irregular war, and this kind of war has its own laws. It wasn't that way. You can't solve things so easily.

Gianni Minà: In Europe it's also said the publisher Feltrinelli contributed — without intending to, of course — to leading the CIA to the traces of Che's little group in the woods near Vallegrande. Is there any truth in that?
Fidel Castro: This is the first time, in fact, I have heard that; the

first time I've heard that rumor, that version. There isn't the slightest possibility Feltrinelli did anything that affected the situation. Today the whole history of the matter is known. Many books have been written about it, and I have read them. First of all, there's Che's diary, which I have studied carefully, very carefully. I knew Che very well, and through the diary I was able to see each of his states of mind, each thing, because I knew him so well.

Then there are all the documents written by the Bolivian army, detailing the information they were receiving: when, at what point, how they interpreted it, what they did. This whole story has been written, and not just by revolutionaries. In addition, there are the diaries of other comrades who survived, of those who were with Che until the final moments, diaries that fell into the hands of the Bolivian army. We know the testimony, we know step by step what occurred. There were a few lapses in discipline, some acts of poor judgment that gave the enemy indications something was going on, although they didn't know the magnitude. But this had nothing to do with Feltrinelli or with anybody, really. These facts are known in minute detail.

There is one thing. They already had camps set up, they had created all the conditions; these are facts that have been told before. The army managed to determine there was something strange going on, but this coincided with other circumstances. Che began an incursion with a large detachment to explore the terrain and make a broad sweep through the area. They left the newest people in camp, those who had just arrived. But the trip lasted several weeks; it turned unto a veritable odyssey. Che's diary describes in detail how they confronted high mountains, harsh terrain, swollen rivers. They also suffered some losses on the trip — some drownings, one or two casualties.

The troops returned completely exhausted after several weeks on the march. When they returned to the camp they discovered there had been some problems in Che's absence — some infractions of discipline, some difficulties. But the worst was that although the troops were worn out, with a few men ill, they had no time to recover. In a few short days the army began to carry out some explorations and the first fighting took place. Because of their experience, Che's men suffered no losses. In fact, ambushes they set with a few men captured weapons and dealt the adversary a hard blow.

But I would say all this happened prematurely. They made another incursion, again leaving a force behind in the camp. This produced a division into two groups that were never to make contact with one another again. Moreover, Che didn't have enough medicine for his asthma. It was the same thing that had happened on the *Granma*, where there was no medicine. In the Sierra Maestra we really had to make an exceptional effort to get Che medicine at any cost, because the terrible asthma attacks paralyzed him. He was in great need of the medicine, but during this whole period he went without it.

All this is described in Che's diary with great rigor, precision, and narrative quality. Each event is described very clearly. This was quite a feat, because they spent months evading and fighting the army. These were not the circumstances for discussing the idea of a support column. Nobody knew where they were. All communications had been cut by the enemy. In the cities the contact points were under constant observation.

At that moment the fate of the guerrilla unit depended on what they themselves did. Che believed his guerrilla unit of 20 men could survive if they relocated, as he proposed, to a place with a social base, where Inti and Coco Peredo were known. That is where they were headed in this final stage. Che knew this was their best chance.

From the description of everything that took place — not only from his diary but also the accounts of the Bolivian army — the feat they did accomplish is impressive, including the number of battles they waged against the army. What they accomplished was of epic proportions. All this is well known.

What could have influenced him? I have an opinion. I think he was deeply affected by the death of the other group. We had news of their death from wire service dispatches. They described how it happened. From our own experience we concluded at once that the news was exact, correct, and truthful. Tamara, Joaquín, the whole unit had been killed. But Che resisted believing it. You can see from his diary he resisted believing it for months. He thought it was another lie by the army, because they had put out a number of false reports. For our part, however, when we saw the dispatches we were immediately convinced it was true.

When he was really convinced — because nearly all his efforts and many of their marches were aimed at trying to make contact with the other unit — when he was really persuaded they no longer existed and he was not going to meet up with them, that is when he began the march toward an area with a social base. By this time he already had some good Bolivian cadres who had distinguished themselves. It was the correct decision; he did have a chance to survive.

How much did the death of the other comrades affect his state of mind? I believe at the end he acted with a certain recklessness. They were walking along a road and at one point he stopped on high ground and said: "Radio Bemba [word of mouth] has been here ahead of us, everyone is expecting us." That's more or less what he said. You can read it in his diary. They were walking along a road toward the area, a public road, when he reached a ridge and wrote in his diary: "Our arrival is being announced by Radio Bemba." That is, everyone was waiting for them.

I think the certainty that Joaquín's unit had been killed influenced his state of mind. I knew him well, I knew how strongly he felt things, and I think in that moment he was acting in conformity with his nature, with a certain degree of recklessness.

He continued to advance, entered the town in daylight, and found it empty. An empty town is a sign that something is up. The people sense a battle is going to take place. Any army — any army in the world! — under those circumstances has only to wait somewhere along the road and set an ambush. And on one of those barren hills, in full light of day, the advance guard began to march as though the army didn't exist. It fell into an ambush in broad daylight, and several men were killed. It was a very serious blow.

The group was also carrying some sick men, including a sick doctor. Che insisted on carrying them even though it held up their movement. Sometimes we ourselves, in similar situations, sought a place where we could leave a sick person — someone who could no longer march — with someone who could take care of them. Che must have been looking for such a possibility. But he had already lost his advance guard. They had been spotted and trapped in a valley, and the dead included some of the good people among the Bolivians. Among the dead was one of the two Peredo brothers who had distinguished themselves so much as Bolivian cadres.

The attack left Che in a very difficult situation in difficult terrain. He had managed to evade the army for months while fighting constantly. He had carried out a feat of epic proportions. But he now found himself in an extremely critical situation. He had been spotted, attacked, and wounded. His rifle had been destroyed. He was taken prisoner and moved to a nearby place.

I would say that even when he was marching along the road with 20 men, including a few Bolivian cadres, that had they made it to the area they sought, they would have had possibilities not just of surviving but of developing the guerrilla movement. Up until that time, to judge by all Che knew and the experience we had, that possibility existed. The moment in which things really changed was when they advanced in broad daylight along a public road in those barren hills where the advance guard was ambushed.

So he must have been greatly influenced by something: his scorn for death — sometimes it seemed as though he went looking for death, at least at certain moments. In such circumstances he really should have advanced more cautiously, gotten off the road, looked for other places. And they should have traveled by night. The ambush, had it been carried out at night, would not have inflicted such great damage. The enemy would have been shooting in the dark, and they might have been spotted by a light or some other indication. I believe that at that moment certain elements in Che's character influenced events.

I knew him very well, and I have read his diary carefully more than once.

Gianni Minà: At this stage was there anything you could have done to assist him? I mean, in this final stage of his epic struggle?

Fidel Castro: It was impossible. What could we have done? Sent a battalion, a company, a regular army? The laws of guerrilla warfare are different; everything depends on what the guerrilla unit itself does. They really did carry out an epic struggle. Some day their accomplishments will be recounted more objectively. The Bolivian army itself in its descriptions... There was one general, General Gary Prado, I read his book [*How I captured Che*]. It reflects the official point of view, but he doesn't conceal his admiration for his adversary.

Clashes with the army occurred a number of times. He knew what to do just as we did. When we arrived in the Sierra we too were dispersed, we managed to gather together seven rifles. We began the struggle again in the Sierra Maestra, where we knew no one, with seven rifles. When we had reached 20 men, we were a force to be reckoned with. Che had confidence in the possibilities of irregular struggle, he knew how to do it.

In such circumstances the guerrilla unit depends on itself. It can neither expect nor receive help from abroad; such assistance is practically impossible. It wasn't possible, and secret assistance wasn't possible either: the entire network of support had been broken up. At that moment everything depended on their own actions. That's why formulas of conventional warfare, speculation about columns that set out, that come and go, don't apply here. All that belongs to the realm of fantasy.

Gianni Minà: President Castro, at the dramatic moment of Che's death a story about you circulated in Europe. It speculated that after the summit meeting in Glassboro in New Jersey between Soviet Premier Kosygin and U.S. President Johnson, the United States and the Soviet Union decided to reach a truce in Asia and Latin America. And that is why Cuba was unable to do anything more to help Che in Bolivia.

Fidel Castro: I am astounded at the number of rumors and fantasies that circulate in Europe. I'm going to begin believing Europe is the least informed area of the world.

Gianni Minà: That may be.

Fidel Castro: I really don't even remember that meeting. The war in Vietnam was at its peak, and Che's action was under way. Neither had anything to do with the other. There was no Soviet participation in this, there was no question of strategy that was being discussed. Really, what it amounted to was that with great loyalty we gave Che the assistance he asked for, the comrades he asked for, the collaboration he asked for, everything. We stood by our word.

What is it that we would have preferred? That Che wait. We would have preferred that he wait until a developed guerrilla front had been established, but we couldn't impose such a decision on him.

We knew we might face political problems, state problems, denunciations, everything of that sort. But we accepted that type of inconvenience so as to fulfill our pledge to him. We respected that commitment. Not only did we respect it, we believed in what he was doing, and we believed he could carry out what he proposed.

I have always said that success or failure is not what indicates whether a line is correct. We all could have died during our struggle; we were on the verge of death many times. If we had died, many people would have said we were wrong. But I think if we had died, it would not have proved we were wrong. I think our road was correct. A series of elements, of imponderables, intervened — including luck — and we almost miraculously survived those difficult days. That would be another long story. But in such circumstances you can't say success is the measure of whether or not a line is correct. Certain factors led to an adverse result, but I don't question the correctness of Che's line. What I say is that I would have preferred he avoid the initial highly dangerous stage, that he join the group as political and military leader, as strategist in a movement that had passed the early stage.

Because of Che's courage, his qualities, his importance, in our war we gave him the most important missions. We didn't give him this mission. The idea, the plan, everything, was his. We shared in it with him because we thought his ideas were correct. He could have done it. He could have done it! I am not going to conclude that because certain factors exerted influence, resulting in the elimination of the guerrilla unit and the death of Che — I am not going to conclude because of this that his course was wrong. You cannot measure the correctness of a line by success or failure. That, in my opinion, would be a mistaken criterion.

That's not the only example. We have seen another case, that of [Francisco] Caamaño, also a man of the highest courage, who could not overcome his impatience to return to his country [the Dominican Republic] and did do so. I talked with him a great deal, I knew him well.

I know then of two cases of great cadres whose impatience led them to their deaths. It's not simply death that is at issue here, the sadness death brings. It is rather that two great cadres, two great revolutionaries, died in this way. And Caamaño with fewer possibilities than Che. Caamaño was a good soldier and well trained. But conditions were also difficult and the group was very small. We would have preferred that these valued cadres be preserved for a more opportune moment.

We did not impose our point of view on them, nor did we prohibit their courageous actions. We had excellent relations of friendship and of trust. Che gave great attention to my point of view and to the opinions I expressed, because we maintained a deep and trusting friendship up until the end. It was his idea. Forbidding him to carry it out was outside the type of relations we had. Not even for reasons of state would I impose an opinion on him.

What we did was help him. We helped something we thought was possible. We would not have been able to help something we thought was impossible, something in which we did not believe, because it would have been our duty to tell him: it's not possible, we can't do that, we can't sacrifice comrades on this mission. But he did what he did. I shared in it and I believed in it.

There is only one thing I would have done differently. He should have waited until a strong movement had developed before a cadre of his quality and strategic importance joined the struggle. He should not have gone through the initial stage. This is the most difficult and dangerous phase, as the facts showed, and it resulted in his death.

Gianni Minà: Why didn't the Bolivian authorities ever return Che's body? Did he still scare them even following his death?

Fidel Castro: They wanted to get rid of Che's body to prevent the establishment of a site that would be venerated and visited by people.

We still don't know what they did with body of Che, or where it is. This has never been clarified. Many of his things, belongings, have surfaced. We know everything that happened, from the accounts of both sides, which agree on most points. What we still don't know is where Che was buried. They wanted him to disappear. The Yankees also wanted him to disappear.

Nonetheless, Che has become a great symbol for the entire world, the perfect example of the heroic and revolutionary man. He became, I would add, one of the most outstanding examples of the combatant and revolutionary in the Third World, and perhaps in the industrialized world as well. And this idea, this image of Che, is not without justification.

Gianni Minà: There's a striking coincidence linked to Che's death. Sixteen or seventeen persons directly or indirectly responsible for his murder in Bolivia have died, not always in the clearest of circumstances.

Fidel Castro: It does seem there have been people who played a part in his murder who have died this way. The likelihood is that no one organized it, that it's simply the people's spontaneous action, bringing to justice those who acted in a contemptible way. I'm not referring to the soldiers who fought against him, but rather to people who served as informers, traitors, and henchmen.

Gianni Minà: Down to the peasant who...

Fidel Castro: I think his name was Honorato.

Gianni Minà: Honorato Rojas.

Fidel Castro: I read about that in the book written by the Bolivian general, Gary Prado, a man who has become something of an invalid. I understand he is now in Washington as military attaché. He wrote a very objective and respectful book, although of course it also has high praise for the Bolivian army. But I'm not going to deny him, a Bolivian soldier, this sentiment toward his institution. The Bolivian army was poorly trained. It was acquiring more experience during that period, this is indisputable. The Yankees made a considerable effort, they intensified their training plans, because they wanted to destroy Che.

Gianni Minà: Two people as reserved as you and Che, how did you greet each other the last time you saw each other? With the hug of old friends, or with a handshake?

Fidel Castro: We saw each other many times. Very warmly and with much affection. No, a hug, without much effusiveness, because we are not very effusive. He wasn't, I'm not. But we feel things deeply. And with great trust. We talked many times. I went to see him several times while he was training the group. They spent months in the province of Pinar del Río.

Gianni Minà: And the day he left?

Fidel Castro: The day he left I went so far as to play a joke. The day he left for good I invited a number of members of the party leadership, the most trusted comrades, to lunch with a visitor. The visitor was Che, disguised. Absolutely no one recognized him in the disguise that had been created. Che had lunch with a few others at a house here in Havana the day before he left — and none of those comrades recognized him either. We had to tell the comrades who came for lunch that it was Che. So as you can see he was very well prepared when he left; nobody recognized him. It was really perfect. Nobody recognized him, not even his closest comrades, who were talking with him the way they would talk with a guest. So we went so far as to play jokes such as this on the comrades the day before he left.

Gianni Minà: I thank you for all you have told me. I believe I had the pleasure of hearing in your words some of the history of our times, of what we are living, thinking, or have hoped. This is something I want to thank you for.

Fidel Castro: We have the obligation to be just. There is no reason to make accusations. We all have things we're sufficiently responsible for, but Monje's responsibility, the other... Well, that's why I explained the story to you in detail.

And that is why I wrote the introduction, what I called a necessary introduction, when we published the [Bolivian] diary of Che. I explained everything, with many more details and the role of everyone involved. I wrote the introduction to explain a series of things, and we published it widely. Later the diary circulated throughout the world. We have such a duty to be objective.

I think I know quite well everything that happened. I have thought a great deal about it, analyzed all the documents, and I think I knew Che quite well; I knew him very, very, very well. I am very sure as to the facts, how they occurred, and what factors may have influenced the course of events.

This is something I have never spoken of before. There are still many chapters of history to be written. What is missing is someone to write them, because those who can write them don't have the time to do so.

Chapter seven

The following speech was given by Fidel Castro on October 8, 1987, at the main ceremony marking the 20th anniversary of the death of Ernesto Che Guevara. The ceremony was held at a newly completed electronic components factory in the city of Pinar del Río.

NEARLY 20 YEARS AGO, on October 18, 1967, we met in Revolution Plaza with a huge crowd to honor comrade Ernesto Che Guevara. Those were very bitter, very difficult days when we received news of the developments in Vado del Yeso, in Yuro Ravine, when news agencies reported Che had fallen in battle.

It didn't take long to realize that those reports were absolutely correct, for they consisted of news items and photos that proved it beyond doubt. For several days the news was coming in, until with all that information in hand — although many of the details we know today were not known at the time — we held the large mass rally, the solemn ceremony in which we paid our last respects to the fallen comrade.

Nearly 20 years have passed since that time, and now, on October 8, we are marking the date he fell in battle. According to reliable reports we have now, he was actually murdered the following day, after having been captured unarmed and wounded; his weapon had been rendered useless in battle. That's why it has become a tradition to commemorate that dramatic event on October 8.

The first year passed and then 5, 10, 15, and now 20 years, and it was necessary to recall the historic dimensions of that development, and particularly the person. Thus in a natural way, rather than a very deliberate or pondered way, the entire people have been recalling the date in recent months. It was possible to commemorate the 20th anniversary on a solemn note as we have seen here today: the playing of taps, the march, the magnificent poem by Nicolas Guillen, which rang out with the same voice we heard 20 years ago.

I could try to give a very solemn, grandiloquent speech, perhaps a written speech, but in these times the pressure of work barely leaves a minute free for thinking more carefully about all those events and the things I could say here, let alone for writing a speech.

That's why I'd prefer to recall Che, share my thoughts with you, because I've thought a lot about Che.

I did an interview, part of which was made public yesterday in our country, in answer to the questions of an Italian journalist [Gianni Minà] who had me in front of the television cameras nearly 16 hours straight. There were more than 100 questions on a variety of subjects, but the journalist was very interested in talking about Che, and between 3:00 a.m. and 4:00 a.m. we got to the subject. I made an effort to answer each of his questions, and I made a special effort to summarize my memories of Che.

I told him how I felt, and I think many comrades feel the same way, regarding Che's permanent presence. We must keep in mind the special relationship with Che, the affection, the fraternal bonds of comradeship, the united struggle over nearly 12 years, from the moment we met in Mexico until the end, a period rich in historic events, some of which have been made public only in the last couple of days.

It was a period filled with heroic and glorious deeds, from the time Che joined us to go on the *Granma* expedition, the landing, the setbacks, the most difficult days, the resumption of the struggle in the mountains, rebuilding an army virtually from scratch, the first clashes, and the last battles.

Then the intense period that followed the victory of the revolution: the first revolutionary laws, in which we were absolutely loyal to the commitments we'd made to the people, carrying out a really radical transformation in the life of the country. There were the things that followed, one after another, such as the start of imperialist hostility; the slander campaigns against the revolution as soon as we started to do justice to the criminals and thugs who had murdered thousands of our fellow citizens; the economic blockade; the Bay of Pigs invasion; the proclamation of the socialist nature of the revolution; the struggle against the mercenaries; the October [Missile] Crisis; the first steps in the construction of socialism when there was nothing — neither experience nor cadres nor engineers nor economists and hardly any technicians, when we were left almost without doctors because 3,000 of the 6,000 doctors in the country left.

Then came the First and Second Declarations of Havana, the start of the isolation imposed on our country, the collective rupture of diplomatic relations by all Latin American governments except Mexico. It was a period in which, along with all these developments, we had to organize the economy of the country. It was a relatively brief but fruitful period replete with unforgettable events.

It must be kept in mind that Che persisted in an old desire, an old idea: to return to South America, to his country, to make the revolution based on the experience he had gained in our country. We should recall the clandestine way in which his departure had to be organized, the barrage of slanders against the revolution, when there was talk of conflicts, of differences with Che, that Che had disappeared. It was even said that he had been murdered because of splits in the ranks of the revolution.

Meanwhile, the revolution calmly and firmly endured the ferocious attack, because over and above the irritation and bitterness caused by those campaigns, the important thing was for Che to be able to fulfill his goals; the important thing was to ensure his safety and that of the compatriots with him on his historic missions.

In the interview I explained the origin of that idea, how when he joined us he had set only one condition: that once the revolution was made, when he wanted to return to South America he would not be prevented from doing so for reasons of state or for the state's convenience, that he would not be held back. We told him he could go ahead and that we would support him. He would remind us of this pledge every so often until the time came when he decided it was time to leave.

Not only did we keep the promise of agreeing to his departure, but we gave him all the help we could. We tried to delay the departure a little. We gave him other tasks to enrich his guerrilla experience, and we tried to create a minimum of conditions so that he would not have to go through the most difficult stage of the first days of organizing a guerrilla force, something we knew full well from our own experience.

We were well aware of Che's talent, his experience, and his role. He was a cadre suited to major strategic tasks and we felt it might be better if other comrades undertook the initial organizational work and that he join at a more advanced stage in the process. This also fitted in with our policy during the war of saving cadres, as they distinguished themselves, for increasingly important and strategic assignments. We did not have many experienced cadres, and as they distinguished themselves we would not send them out every day with a squad to ambush; rather, we gave them more important tasks in keeping with their ability and experience.

Thus, I remember that during the days of Batista's final offensive in the Sierra Maestra mountains against our militant but small forces, the most experienced cadres were not in the front lines; they were assigned strategic leadership assignments and saved for our devastating counterattack. It would have been pointless to put Che, Camilo [Cienfuegos], and other comrades who had participated in many battles at the head of a squad. We held them back so that they could subsequently lead columns that would undertake risky missions of great importance, and it was then that we did send them into enemy territory with full responsibility and awareness of the risks, as in the case of the invasion of Las Villas led by Camilo and Che. This was an extraordinarily difficult assignment that required men of great experience and authority as column commanders, men capable of reaching the goal.

In line with this reasoning, and considering the objectives, perhaps it would have been better if this principle had been observed and Che had joined at a later stage. It really was not so critical for him to handle everything right from the start. But he was impatient, very impatient really. Some Argentinian comrades had been killed in the initial efforts he had made years before, including Ricardo Massetti, the founder of Prensa Latina. He remembered that often and was really impatient to start to participate.

As always, we respected our commitments and his views, for our relationship was always based on absolute trust, absolute brotherhood, regardless of our ideas about what the right time for him to join in would be. And so we gave him all the help and all the facilities possible to start the struggle.

Then news came of the first clashes and contact was completely lost. The enemy detected the initial stage of organization of the guerrilla movement, and this marked the start of a period lasting many months in which almost the only news we received was what came via international news dispatches, and we had to know how to interpret them. But that's something our revolution has become very experienced at: determining when a report is reliable or when it is made up, false.

I remember, for example, when a dispatch came with the news of the death of Joaquín's group (his real name was Vilo Acuña). When we analyzed it, I immediately concluded that it was true; this was because of the way they described how the group had been eliminated while crossing a river. Because of our own guerrilla experience, because of what we had lived through, we knew how a small guerrilla group can be done away with. We knew the few, exceptional ways such a group can be destroyed.

When it was reported that a peasant had made contact with the army and provided detailed information on the location and plans of the group, which was looking for a way to cross the river; how the army set up an ambush on the other bank at a spot on the route the same peasant had told the guerrilla fighters to use; the way the army opened fire in midstream. There was no doubt as to the truth of the explanation. If the writers of false reports, which came in often, tried to do it again, it was impossible that they, who were always so clumsy in their lies, would have had enough intelligence and experience to make up the exact circumstances in which the group could be eliminated. That's why we concluded the report was true.

As we have explained, we had hopes that even with only 20

men left, even in a very difficult situation, the guerrillas still had a chance. They were headed toward an area where the peasants were organized, where some good Bolivian cadres had influence, and until that moment, until almost the very end, there was a chance that the movement could be consolidated and could develop.

The circumstances in which my relationship with Che developed were so unique — the almost unreal history of the brief but intense saga of the first years of the revolution when we were used to making the impossible possible — that, as I explained to that journalist, one often had the impression that Che had not died, that he was still alive. Since his was such an exemplary personality, so unforgettable, so familiar, it was difficult to resign oneself to the idea of his death.

Sometimes I would dream — all of us dream of things related to our lives and struggles — that I saw Che, that he returned, that he was alive. How often this happened! I told the journalist that these are feelings you seldom talk about, but they give an idea of the impact of Che's personality and also of the extraordinary degree to which he really lives on, almost as if his were a physical presence, with his ideas and deeds, with his example and all the things he created, with his continued relevance and the respect for him not only in Latin America but in Europe and all over the world.

As we predicted on October 18, some 20 years ago, he became a symbol for all the oppressed, for all the exploited, for all patriotic and democratic forces, for all revolutionaries. He became a permanent and invincible symbol.

We feel Che's presence for all these reasons, because of this real force that he still has today which, even though 20 years have gone by, exists in the spirit of all of us, when we hear the poem, when we hear the march or the bugle sounded before a moment's silence, when we open our newspapers and see photographs of Che during different stages of his life, his image, so well known throughout the world. It has to be said that Che not only had all the virtues and all the human and moral qualities to be a symbol, he also had the appearance of a symbol, the image of a symbol: his look, the frankness and strength of his look; his face, which reflects character, irrepressibly determined for action, at the same time showing great intelligence and great purity — when we hear the poems that have been written, the episodes that are recounted, and the stories that are repeated, we feel the reality of Che's relevance, of his presence.

If one imagines that Che is alive, that he is in action and that he never died, it's not strange if one feels his presence not only in everyday life, but even in dreams. In the end we must reach the conclusion that to all intents and purposes in the life of our revolution Che never died, and in the light of what has been done, he is more alive than ever, and is a more powerful opponent of imperialism than ever.

Those who disposed of his body so that he would not become a symbol; those who, under the guidance of their imperial masters, did not want any trace to remain, have discovered that although there is no body, nevertheless a frightening opponent of imperialism, a symbol, a force, a presence does exist that can never be destroyed.

When they hid Che's body they showed their weakness and their cowardice, because they also showed their fear of the example and the symbol. They did not want the exploited peasants, the workers, the students, the intellectuals, the democrats, the progressives, or the patriots of this hemisphere to have a place to go to pay tribute to Che. And in the world today, in which there is no specific place to go to pay tribute to Che's remains, tribute is paid to him everywhere.

Today tribute is not paid to Che once a year, nor once every 5, 10, 15, or 20 years; today homage is paid to Che every year, every month, every day, everywhere in a factory, in a school, in a military barracks, in a home, among children, among Pioneers. Who can count how many millions of times in these 20 years the Pioneers have said: "Pioneers for communism, we will be like Che!"

This one fact I've just mentioned, this one idea, this one custom in itself constitutes a great and permanent presence of Che. And I think not only our Pioneers, not only our children, but children all over the hemisphere, all over the world could repeat this same slogan: "Pioneers for communism, we will be like Che!"

Really, there can be no superior symbol, there can be no better image, there cannot be a more exact idea, when searching for the model revolutionary person, when searching for the model communist. I say this because I have the deepest conviction — just the same or more so than when I spoke that October 18 and I asked how we wanted our fighters, our revolutionaries, our party members, our children to be, and I said that we wanted them to be like Che. He is the image of that human being if we want to talk about a communist society; if our real objective is to build not just socialism but the higher stages of socialism, if humanity is not going to renounce the lofty and extraordinary idea of living in a communist society one day.

If we need a paradigm, a model, an example to follow to attain these elevated ideas, then people like Che are essential, as are men and women who imitate him, who are like him, who think like him, who act like him; men and women whose conduct resembles his when it comes to doing their duty in every little thing, every detail, every activity; in his attitude toward work, his habit of teaching and educating by setting an example; his attitude of wanting to be first at everything, the first to volunteer for the most difficult tasks, the hardest ones, the most self-sacrificing; the individual who gives his body and soul to a cause, the individual who gives his body and soul for others, the person who displays true solidarity, the individual who never lets down a comrade; the simple person; the person without a flaw, who doesn't live any contradiction between what they say and what they do, between what they practice and what they preach; a man of thought and a man of action — all of which Che symbolizes.

For our country it is a great honor and privilege to have had Che as a son of our people even though he wasn't born in this land. He was a son because he earned the right to consider himself and to be considered a son of our country.

That's not to say that I think exceptional people are rare; that's not to say that amid the masses there are not hundreds, thousands, even millions of exceptional men and women. I said it once during the bitter days after Camilo disappeared. When I recounted the history of how Camilo became the man he was, I said: "Among our people there are many Camilos." I could also say: "Among our peoples of the world there are many Ches."

But, why do we call them exceptional? Because, in actual fact, in the world in which they lived, in the circumstances in which they lived, they had the chance and the opportunity to demonstrate all that human beings, with their generosity and solidarity, are capable of being. And, indeed, seldom do ideal circumstances exist in which human beings have the opportunity to express themselves and to show everything they have inside as was the case with Che.

Of course, it's clear that there are countless men and women among the masses who, partly as a result of other people's examples and certain new values, are capable of heroism, including a kind of heroism I greatly admire: silent heroism, anonymous heroism, silent virtue, anonymous virtue. But given that it's so unusual, so rare for all the necessary circumstances to exist to produce a figure like Che — who today has become a symbol for the world, a symbol that will grow — it is a great honor and privilege that this figure was born during our revolution.

And as proof of what I said earlier about Che's presence and force today, I could ask: could there be a better date, a better anniversary than this one to remember Che with all our conviction and deep feelings of appreciation and gratitude? Is there a better moment than this particular anniversary, when we are in the middle of the rectification process?

What are we rectifying? We're rectifying all those things — and there are many — that strayed from the revolutionary spirit, from revolutionary work, revolutionary virtue, revolutionary effort, revolutionary responsibility; all those things that strayed from the spirit of solidarity among people. We're rectifying all the shoddiness and mediocrity that is precisely the negation of Che's ideas, his revolutionary thought, his style, his spirit, and his example.

I really believe, and I say it with great satisfaction, that if Che were sitting in this chair, he would feel jubilant. He would be happy about what we are doing these days, just like he would have felt very unhappy during that unstable period, that disgraceful period of building socialism in which there began to prevail a series of ideas, of mechanisms, of bad habits, which would have caused Che to feel profound and terrible bitterness.

For example, voluntary work, the brainchild of Che and one of the best things he left us during his stay in our country and his part in the revolution, was steadily on the decline. It became a formality almost. It would be done on the occasion of a special date, a Sunday. People would sometimes run around and do things in a disorganized way.

The bureaucrat's view, the technocrat's view that voluntary work was neither basic nor essential gained more and more ground. The idea was that voluntary work was kind of silly, a waste of time, that problems had to be solved with overtime, with more and more overtime, and this while the regular workday was not even being used efficiently. We had fallen into the bog of bureaucracy, of overstaffing, of work norms that were out of date, the bog of deceit, of untruth. We'd fallen into a whole host of bad habits that Che would have been really appalled at.

If Che had ever been told that one day, under the Cuban revolution there would be enterprises prepared to steal to pretend they were profitable, Che would have been appalled. Or if he'd been told of enterprises that wanted to be profitable and give out prizes, bonuses and I don't know what else, and they'd sell the materials allotted to them to build and charge as though they had built whatever it was, Che would have been appalled.

And I'll tell you that this happened in the 15 municipalities in the capital of the republic, in the 15 enterprises responsible for house repairs; and that's only one example. They'd appear as though what they'd produced was worth 8,000 pesos a year, and when the chaos was done away with, it turned out they were producing 4,000 pesos worth or less. So they were not profitable. They were only profitable when they stole.

Che would have been appalled if he'd been told that enterprises existed that would cheat to fulfill and even surpass their production plan by pretending to have done January's work in December.

Che would have been appalled if he'd been told that there were enterprises that fulfilled their production plan and then distributed prizes for having fulfilled it in value but not in stock, and that engaged in producing items that meant more value and refrained from producing others that yielded less profit, despite the fact that one item without the other was not worth anything.

Che would have been appalled if he'd been told that production norms were so slack, so weak, so immoral that on certain occasions almost all the workers fulfilled them two or three times over.

Che would have been appalled if he'd been told that money was becoming people's concern, their fundamental motivation. He who warned us so much against that would have been appalled. Work shifts were being shortened and millions of hours of overtime reported; the mentality of our workers was being corrupted and were increasingly being motivated by the pesos on their minds.

Che would have been appalled for he knew that communism could never be attained by trekking along those worn capitalist paths and that to follow along those paths would mean eventually to forget all ideas of solidarity and even internationalism. To follow those paths would imply never developing a new human being and a new society.

Che would have been appalled if he'd been told that a day would come when bonuses and more bonuses of all kinds would be paid, without these having anything to do with production.

Were he to have seen a group of enterprises teeming with two-bit capitalists — as we call them — playing at capitalism, beginning to think and act like capitalists, forgetting about the country, the people, and high standards (because high standards just didn't matter; all they cared about was the money being earned thanks to the low norms) he would have been appalled.

And were he to have seen that one day they would not just make manual work subject to production norms — which has a certain logic to it, like cutting cane and doing many other manual and physical activities — but even intellectual work, even radio and television work, and that here even a surgeon's work was likely to be subject to norms — putting just anybody under the knife in order to double or triple his income — I can truthfully say that Che would have been appalled, because none of those paths will ever lead us to communism. On the contrary, those paths lead to all the bad habits and the alienation of capitalism.

Those paths, I repeat — and Che knew it very well — would never lead us to building real socialism, as a first and transitional stage to communism.

But don't think that Che was naive, an idealist, or someone out of touch with reality. Che understood and took reality into consideration. But Che believed in human beings. And if we don't believe in human beings, if we think that they are incorrigible little animals, only capable of advancing if you feed them grass or tempt them with a carrot or whip them with a stick — anybody who believes this, anybody convinced of this will never be a revolutionary; anybody who believes this, anybody convinced of this will never be a socialist; anybody who believes this, anybody convinced of this will never be a communist.

Our revolution is an example of what faith in human beings means because our revolution started from scratch, from nothing. We did not have a single weapon, we did not have a penny, even those who started the struggle were unknown, and yet we confronted all that might. We confronted their hundreds of millions of pesos, we confronted the thousands of soldiers, and the revolution triumphed because we believed in humanity. Not only was victory made possible, but so was confronting the empire and getting this far, only a short way off from celebrating the 29th anniversary of the triumph of the revolution. How could we have done all this if we had not had faith in human beings?

Che had great faith in human beings. Che was a realist and did not reject material incentives. He deemed them necessary during the transitional stage, while building socialism. But Che attached more importance — more and more importance — to the conscious factor, to the moral factor.

Nevertheless, it would be a caricature to believe that Che was unrealistic and unfamiliar with the reality of a society and a people who had just emerged from capitalism.

But Che was mostly known as a person of action, a soldier, a leader, a military figure, a guerrilla, an exemplary person who always was the first in everything; who never asked others to do something that he himself would not do first; a model of someone who was righteous, honest, pure, courageous, and solidarized with his fellow humans. These are the virtures he possessed and the ones we remember him by.

Che was a person of very profound thought, and he had the exceptional opportunity during the first years of the revolution to delve deeply into very important aspects of the building of socialism because, given his qualities, whenever someone was needed to do an important job, Che was always there. He really was a many-sided individual and whatever his assignment, he fulfilled it in a completely serious and responsible manner.

He was in INRA [National Institute of Agrarian Reform] and managed a few industries under its jurisdiction at a time when the main industries had not yet been nationalized and only a few factories had been taken over. He headed the National Bank, another of the responsibilities entrusted to him, and he also headed the Ministry of Industry when this agency was set up. Nearly all the factories had been nationalized by then and everything had to be organized, production had to be maintained, and Che took on the job, as he had taken on many others. He did so with total devotion, working day and night, Saturdays and Sundays, at all hours, and he really set out to solve far-reaching problems. It was then that he tackled the task of applying Marxist-Leninist principles to the organization of production, the way he understood it, the way he saw it.

He spent years doing that; he spoke a lot, wrote a lot on all those subjects, and he really managed to develop a rather elaborate and very profound theory on the manner in which, in his opinion, socialism should be built leading to a communist society.

Recently, all these ideas were compiled, and an economist wrote a book that was awarded a Casa de las Américas prize. The author compiled, studied, and presented in a book the essence of Che's economic ideas, retrieved from many of his speeches and writings — articles and speeches dealing with a subject so decisive in the building of socialism. The name of the book is *Che's economic thought.* So much has been done to recall his other qualities that this aspect, I think, has been largely ignored in our country. Che held truly profound, courageous, bold ideas, which were different from many paths already taken.

In essence — in essence! — Che was radically opposed to using and developing capitalist economic laws and categories in building socialism. He advocated something that I have often insisted on: building socialism and communism is not just a matter of producing and distributing wealth but is also a matter of education and consciousness. He was firmly opposed to using these categories, which have been transferred from capitalism to socialism, as instruments to build the new society.

At a given moment some of Che's ideas were incorrectly interpreted and, what's more, incorrectly applied. Certainly no serious attempt was ever made to put them into practice, and there came a time when ideas diametrically opposed to Che's economic thought began to take over.

This is not the occasion for going deeper into the subject. I'm essentially interested in expressing one idea: today, on the 20th anniversary of Che's death; today, in the midst of the profound rectification process we are all involved in, we fully understand that rectification does not mean extremism, that rectification cannot mean idealism, that rectification cannot imply for any reason whatsoever lack of realism, that rectification cannot even imply abrupt changes.

Starting out from the idea that rectification means, as I've said before, looking for new solutions to old problems, rectifying many negative tendencies that had been developing; that rectification implies making more accurate use of the system and the mechanisms we have now, an Economic Management and Planning System which, as we said at the enterprises meeting, was a horse, a lame nag with many sores that we were treating with mercurochrome and prescribing medicines for, putting splints on one leg. In short, fixing up the nag, the horse. I said that the thing to do now was to go on using that horse, knowing its bad habits, the perils of that horse, how it kicked and bucked, and try to lead it on our path and not go wherever it wishes to take us. I've said, let us take up the reins!

These are very serious, very complicated matters and here we can't afford to take shots in the dark, and there's no place for adventures of any kind. The experience of so many years that quite a few of us have had the privilege of accumulating through a revolutionary process is worth something. And that's why we say now, we cannot fulfill the plan as to value, we must fulfill it as to goods produced. We demand this categorically, and anyone who does otherwise must be sacked, because there's no other choice!

We maintain that all projects must be started and finished quickly so that there is never a repeat of what happened to us on account of the nag's bucking and kicking: that business of doing the earthmoving and putting up a few foundations because that was worth a lot and then not finishing the building because that was worth little; that tendency to say, "I fulfilled my plan as to value but I didn't finish a single building," which made us bury hundreds of millions, billions, and we never finished anything.

It took 14 years to build a hotel! Fourteen years wasting iron bars, sand, stone, cement, rubber, fuel, manpower before the country made a single penny from the hotel being used. Eleven years to finish our hospital here in Pinar del Río! It's true that in the end it was finished and it was finished well. But things of this sort should never happen again.

The minibrigades, which were destroyed for the sake of such mechanisms, are now rising again from their ashes like a phoenix and demonstrating the significance of that mass movement, the significance of that revolutionary path of solving the problems that the theoreticians, technocrats, those who do not believe in human beings, and those who believe in two-bit capitalism had stopped and dismantled. This was how they were leading us into critical situations.

In the capital, where the minibrigades emerged, it pains us to think that over 15 years ago we had found an excellent solution to such a vital problem, and yet they were destroyed in their peak. And so we didn't even have the manpower to build housing in the capital; and the problems kept piling up, tens of thousands of homes were propped up and were in danger of collapsing and killing people.

Now the minibrigades have been reborn and there are more than 20,000 minibrigade members in the capital. They're not in contradiction with the nag, with the Economic Management and Planning System, simply because the factory or workplace that sends them to the construction site pays them, but the state reimburses the factory or workplace for the salary of the minibrigade member. The difference is that whereas the worker would normally work five or six hours, on the minibrigade he works 10, 11, or 12 hours doing the job of two or three people, and the enterprise saves money.

Our two-bit capitalist can't say his enterprise is being ruined. On the contrary, he can say, "They're helping the enterprise. I'm doing the job with 30, 40, or 50 less people and spending less on salaries." He can say, "I'm going to be profitable or at least lose less money; I'll distribute more prizes and bonuses since salary expenditure will be cut down." He organizes production better, he gets housing for his workers, who in turn are happier because they have new housing. He builds community projects such as special schools, polyclinics, childcare centers for the children of working women, for the family; in short, so many extremely useful things we are doing now and the state is building them without spending an additional cent in salaries. That really is miraculous!

We could ask the two-bit capitalists and profiteers who have blind faith in the mechanisms and categories of capitalism: Could you achieve such a miracle? Could you manage to build 20,000 housing units in the capital without spending a cent more on salaries? Could you build 50 childcare centers in a year without spending a cent more on salary, when only five had been planned in five years and they weren't even built and 19,500 mothers were waiting to get their children a place, which never materialized.

It can be seen in the capital today that one in eight workers can be mobilized, I'm sure. This is not necessary because there would not be enough materials to give tasks to 100,000 people working in Havana, each one doing the work of three. We're seeing impressive examples of feats of work, and this is achieved by mass methods, by revolutionary methods, by communist methods, combining the interests of people in need with the interests of factories and those of society as a whole.

I don't want to become the judge of different theories, although I have my own theories and know what things I believe in and what things I don't and can't believe in. These questions are discussed frequently in the world today. And I only ask modestly, during this process of rectification and at this 20th anniversary, is that Che's economic thought be made known; that it be known here, in Latin America, in the world: in the developed capitalist world, in the Third World, and in the socialist world. Let it be known there, too!

In the same way that we read many texts, of all varieties, and many manuals, in the socialist camp, Che's economic thought should be known. Let it be known! I don't say they have to adopt it, we don't have to get involved in that. Everyone must adopt the thought, the theory, the thesis they consider most appropriate, that which best suits them, as judged by each country. I absolutely respect the right of every country to apply the method or systems it considers appropriate; I respect it completely!

I simply ask that in a cultured country, in a cultured world, in a world where ideas are discussed, Che's economic theories should be made known. I especially ask that our students of economics, of whom we have many and who read all kinds of pamphlets, manuals, theories about capitalist categories and capitalist laws, also begin to study Che's economic thought, so as to enrich their knowledge.

It would be a sign of ignorance to believe there is only one way of doing things, arising from the concrete experience of a specific time and specific historical circumstances. What I ask for, what I limit myself to asking for, is a little more knowledge, consisting of knowing about other points of view, points of view as respected, as deserving, and as coherent as Che's point of view.

I can't conceive that our future economists, that our future generations will act, live, and develop like another animal species, in this case like the mule, who has those blinders only so that it can't see to either side; mules, furthermore, with grass and the carrot dangling in front as their only motivation. No, I would like them to read, not only to intoxicate themselves with certain ideas, but also to look at other ones, analyze them, and think about them.

Because if we were talking with Che and we said to him, "Look, all this has happened to us," all those things I was talking about before, what happened to us in construction, in agriculture, in industry, what happened to variety, work quality, and all that, Che would have said, "It's as I said, it's as I said." He'd have said, "It's as I warned, what's happening is exactly what I thought would happen," because that's simply the way it is.

I want our people to be a people of ideas, of concepts. I want them to analyze those ideas, think about them, and, if they want, discuss them. I consider these things to be essential.

It might be that some of Che's ideas are closely linked to the initial stages of the revolution, like the one concerning his belief that when a quota was surpassed, the salary received should not go above that received by those on the scale immediately above, because he wanted the worker to study, and he associated his concept with the idea that people with a very poor education and little technical expertise should study. Today our people are much better educated, more cultured. We could discuss whether now they should earn as much as the next level or more. We could discuss questions associated with our reality of a far more educated people, a people far better prepared technically, although we must never give up the idea of constantly improving ourselves technically and educationally.

But many of Che's ideas are absolutely relevant today, ideas without which I am convinced communism cannot be built, like the idea that human beings should not be corrupted; that they should never be alienated; the idea that without a consciousness, simply producing wealth, socialism as a superior society could not be built, and communism could never be built.

I think that many of Che's ideas — many of his ideas! — have great relevance today. Had we known, had we learned about Che's economic thought we'd be a hundred times more alert, even to ride the horse, and whenever the horse wanted to turn right or left, wherever it wanted to turn — although, mind you, here this was without a doubt a right-wing horse — we should have pulled it up hard and got it back on the track, and whenever it refused to move, use the spurs hard.

I think a rider, that is to say, an economist, a party cadre, an administrative cadre, armed with Che's ideas would be better equipped to lead the horse along the right track. Just being familiar with Che's thought, just knowing his ideas would enable them to say, "I'm doing badly here, I'm doing badly there, that's a consequence of this or the other," provided that the system and mechanisms for building socialism and communism are really being developed and improved.

I say this because it is my deepest conviction that if we ignore his thought it will be difficult to get very far, to achieve real socialism, really revolutionary socialism, socialism with socialists, socialism and communism with communists. I'm absolutely convinced that ignoring those ideas would be a crime. That's what I'm putting to you.

We have enough experience to know how to do things; and there are extremely valuable principles of immense worth in Che's ideas and thought that simply go beyond the image that many people have of Che as a brave, heroic, pure man, of Che as a saint because of his virtues, as a martyr because of his selflessness and heroism. Che was also a revolutionary, a thinker, a person of doctrine, a person of great ideas, who was capable with great consistency of working out instruments and principles that unquestionably are essential to the revolutionary path.

Capitalists are very happy when they hear people talk about rent, profit, interest, bonuses, superbonuses; when they hear about markets, supply and demand as elements that regulate production and promote quality, efficiency, and all those things. For they say, "That's my kind of talk, that's my philosophy, that's my doctrine," and the emphasis that socialism may place on them makes them happy, for they know these are essential aspects of capitalist theory, laws, and categories.

We ourselves are being criticized by quite a few capitalists; they try to make people think that the Cuban revolutionaries are unrealistic, that the thing to do is go for all the decoys of capitalism, and then they aim their guns at us for that reason. We'll see how far we get, even riding on the old nag full of sores, but correctly led, for as long as we don't have anything better than the old nag. We'll see how far we get in the rectification process with the steps we're taking now.

That's why on this, the 20th anniversary, I'm making an appeal for our party members, our youth, our students, our economists to study and familiarize themselves with Che's political and economic thought.

Che is a figure with enormous prestige. Che is a figure whose influence will grow. Needless to say, those who feel frustrated or who dare to fight Che's ideas or use certain terms to describe Che or depict him as naive, as someone who is out of touch with reality, do not deserve any revolutionary's respect. That's why we want our youth to have that instrument, to wield that weapon, even if for the time being it only serves to say, don't follow that mistaken path foreseen by Che; even if it only serves to increase our knowledge; even if it only serves to force us to meditate or to delve deeper into our revolutionary thought.

I sincerely believe that more than this ceremony, more than formal activities, more than all the honors, what we do is really the best homage we can pay Che. The work spirit that is starting to appear in so many places and that is evident in so many examples in this province: those workers in Viñales who are working 12 and 14 hours building minidams, starting them and finishing them one right after the other, and building them at half what they otherwise would have cost, to the extent that it could be said that in comparison with other projects. Were we to use a capitalist term — although Che was opposed even to using capitalist terms when analyzing questions of socialism — were we to use the term profitability, we could say that those men on the minidam construction brigade working in Viñales are more than 100 percent profitable.

Che devoted absolute, total, priority attention to accounting, to analyzing expenditures and costs, cent by cent. Che could not conceive of building socialism and running the economy without proper organization, efficient control, and strict accounting of every cent. Che could not conceive of development without an increase in labor productivity. He even studied mathematics to use mathematical formulas for economic checks and to measure the efficiency of the economy. What's more, Che even dreamed of computers being used in running the economy as a key factor to measure efficiency under socialism .

And those workers I mentioned have made a contribution: for every peso spent they produce two; for every million pesos spent they produce two million. They and those working on the

Guamá Dam, those working on the canal, those working on the thruway to Pinar del Río, those who are going to work on the Patate Dam, those who have started to work on roads and the waterworks in the city — there are a number of groups of workers who are undertaking real feats with pride, honor, discipline, loyalty to work. They are working with great productivity.

Fortunately, during these years we have trained a large number of people with a high degree of technical knowledge and experience, university graduates and intermediate-level technicians. How does this compare to what we had in the early years of the revolution? When Che headed the Ministry of Industry, how many engineers did the country have, how many technicians, designers, researchers, scientists? Now we have about 20 times the number we had then, perhaps more. If he had been able to draw on the collective experience of all the cadres that we have now, who knows what he could have accomplished.

Let's look at the medical sector alone. Back then we had 3,000 doctors and now we have 28,000. Each year our 21 medical schools graduate as many doctors as the total number in the country at that time. What a privilege! What a power! What force! As of next year we'll be graduating more doctors than those who stayed in the country in the early years. Can we or can we not do what we set our minds to in the field of public health? And what doctors they are! They work in the countryside, in the mountains, or in Nicaragua, Angola, Mozambique, Ethiopia, Vietnam, Kampuchea, or the end of the world! Those are the doctors trained by the revolution!

I'm sure Che would be proud, not of the shoddy things that have been done with such a two-bit profiteering mentality; he'd be proud of the knowledge and technology our people have, of our teachers who went to Nicaragua and the 100,000 who offered to go. He'd be proud of our doctors willing to go anywhere in the world, of our technicians, of our hundreds of thousands of compatriots who have been on internationalist missions.

I'm sure Che would be proud of that spirit just like we all are, but what we have built with our heads and hearts cannot be destroyed with our feet. That's the point, that and the fact that with all the resources that we have built up, with all that force, we should be able to advance and take advantage of all the potential opened up by socialism and the revolution to get people to move ahead. I would like to know if the capitalists have people like those I mentioned.

They are extraordinary internationalists and workers; you have to talk to them to see how they think and feel, to see how deeply they love their work, and this is not because they're workaholics but because they feel the need to make up for lost time, time lost during the revolution, time lost during almost 60 years of neocolonial republic, time lost during centuries of colonialism.

We must regain this time! And hard work is the only way, not waiting 100 years to build 100 childcare centers in the capital when we can really do it in two; not waiting 100 years to build 350 all over the country when we can do it in three; not waiting 100 years to solve the housing problem when we can do it in a few years, our stones, our sand, our materials, our cement, even with our oil and steel produced by our workers.

As I said this afternoon at the hospital ceremony, the year 2000 is just around the corner. We must set ourselves ambitious goals for the year 2000, not for the year 3000 or 2100 or 2050, and if someone suggests that we should, we must reply: "That may suit you but not us! We have the historic mission of building a new country, a new society, the historic mission of making a revolution and developing a country; those of us who have had the honor and privilege of not just promoting development but a socialist development and working for a more humane and advanced society."

To those who encourage laziness and frivolity we will say, "We will live longer than you, not just better than you, or like we would live if everyone were like you. We will live longer than you and be healthier than you because with your laziness you will be sedentary and obese, you will have heart problems, circulatory ailments, and all sorts of other things, because work doesn't harm your health, work promotes health, work safeguards health, and work created humanity."

These men and women doing great things must become

models. We could say that they're being true to the motto, "We will be like Che!" They are working like Che worked or as Che would have worked.

When we were discussing where this ceremony should be held, there were many possible places. It could have been in Revolution Plaza in the capital, it could have been in a province, it could have been in one of the many workplaces or factories that the workers wanted to name after Che.

We gave the matter some thought and recalled this new and important factory, the pride of Pinar del Río, the pride of the country and example of what can be done with progress, study, education in this province, which in the past was so neglected and backward and now has workers capable of running such a complex and sophisticated factory. We need only say that the rooms where the circuits are printed must be 10 times cleaner than an operating room to meet the required standard. It was necessary to do such complex work, with such quality and good equipment, and Pinar del Río residents are doing it marvelously.

When we toured it we were deeply impressed and we talked with many comrades, the members of the Central Committee, about what you were doing in the factory; in the machine industry, which is advancing at a rapid pace; what was being done in construction. We realized the great future of this factory as a manufacturer of components, of vanguard technology, which will have a major impact on development and productivity, on the automation of production processes. When we toured your first-rate factory and saw the ideas you had which are being put into practice, we realized it will become a huge complex of many thousands of workers, the pride of the province and the pride of the country. In the next five years more than 100 million pesos will be invested in it to make it a real giant. When we learned that the workers wanted to name it after Che because he was so concerned with electronics, computers, and mathematics, the leadership of the party decided that this was where the ceremony marking the 20th anniversary of Che's death should be held, and that the factory should be given the glorious and beloved name of Ernesto Che Guevara.

I know that its workers, its young workers, its dozens and

dozens of engineers, its hundreds of technicians will do honor to that name and work as they should. This doesn't mean being here 14, 12, or 10 hours, for often on certain jobs eight hours of work well done is a real feat. We've seen comrades, especially many women workers doing microsoldering, which is really difficult work that requires tremendous rigor and concentration. We've seen them, and it's hard to imagine how they can spend eight hours doing that work and turn out up to 5,000 units daily.

Comrades don't think that we feel that the way to solve problems is to work 12 or 14 hours a day. There are jobs where you can't work 12 or 14 hours. In some even eight can be too much. One day we hope that not all workdays will be the same. We hope that in certain fields — if we have enough personnel, and we will if we employ them efficiently — we can have six-hour workdays.

What I mean to say is that being true to Che's example and name also means using the workday with the right pace, being concerned about high standards, having people do various tasks, avoiding overstaffing, working in an organized manner, and developing consciousness.

I'm sure that the workers of this factory will be worthy of Che's name, just as I'm sure that this province was deserving of hosting the anniversary and will continue to be deserving.

If there is something left to say tonight it's that despite our problems; despite the fact that we have less hard currency than ever before, for reasons we have explained in the past; despite the drought; despite the intensification of the imperialist blockade — as I see our people respond, as I see more and more possibilities open up, I feel confident, I feel optimistic, and I am absolutely convinced that we will do everything we set our minds to!

We'll do it with the people, with the masses; we'll do it with the principles, pride, and honor of each and every one of our party members, workers, youth, peasants, and intellectuals!

I can proudly say that we are giving Che well-deserved tribute and honor, and if he lives more than ever, so will the homeland! If he is an opponent of imperialism more powerful than ever, the homeland will also be more powerful than ever against imperialism and its rotten ideology! And if one day we chose the path of revolution, of socialist revolution and of communism, the path of building communism, today we are prouder to have chosen that path because it is the only one that can give rise to others like Che and a people composed of millions of men and women capable of being like Che!

As [José] Martí said, whereas there are people without dignity, there are people who carry inside them the dignity of many people! We might add that there are people who carry inside them the dignity of the world, and one of those is Che!

Postscript

The campaign to divide the ideas and personalities of Che Guevara and Fidel Castro has never really ceased. The colors and configurations may change, but a constant in the 35-year history of the Cuban revolution has been the campaign to separate the image and example of Che Guevara from the Cuban revolution itself.

Who better than Fidel Castro to respond to this campaign. This selection of writings, interviews and speeches by Fidel Castro is the closest to a memoir of Guevara that so far exists. It is a revealing portrait not just of the subject but of the author as well.

Understanding the Cuban revolution in its own context and recognizing its unique characteristics — not with fixed schemas — is the challenge facing all those who seek to analyze and study Cuba. It is in this spirit that Castro reflects on Guevara, in the political context of their collaborative years. Most recently, in a 1992 interview with Nicaragua's Tomás Borge published in the book Face to face with Fidel Castro, *Castro was asked why there had been the revival of interest in Che's writing in Cuba. The Cuban leader observed:*

We have always paid a lot of attention to Che's thinking in Cuba. I myself have kept his thinking increasingly in mind, ever since we began our process of rectification, long before all those problems arose in the socialist camp and perestroika appeared on the horizon. I remember that we were observing an anniversary of Che's death — I think it was the 20th anniversary — and I spoke at length about Che and all these matters.

My admiration and fellow feeling for Che have grown as I have seen what has happened in the socialist camp, because he was categorically opposed to the use of capitalist methods for the construction of socialism. One of our comrades, an economist, gathered together all of the ideas Che set forth in this regard in his writings and speeches, and he compiled and arranged them. They are of enormous value and should be studied, because I think that the use of those capitalist methods and categories had an alienating influence in the socialist countries.

You were asking about what caused the failure of socialism in those countries.

I think that Che had a prophetic vision when, as early as the first few years of the 1960s, he foresaw all of the drawbacks and consequences of the method that was being used to construct socialism in Eastern Europe.

He said there was no need to resort to those methods and to that capitalist philosophy. At one time, we began to use economic planning and management methods that were copied from the European socialist experience. Those concepts began to prevail because of the enormous prestige the Soviet Union and the other socialist countries had in Cuba and because of the idealistic mistakes we made in the first few years of the revolution. This created a culture favorable to the appearance and application in Cuba of the methods for the construction of socialism that were being applied in the Soviet Union and other socialist countries.

I have always made a distinction between the Soviet Union and the other countries, because socialism wasn't built exclusively with those methods in the Soviet Union. I'm referring mainly to the smaller countries in the socialist camp, because the development programs in the Soviet Union were very powerful, and the main decisions that made the Soviet Union's great economic growth possible weren't associated with income-yield capacity in the capitalist sense or any other such categories.

That philosophy was applied in our country. After 10 or 11 years, while we were waiting to see its results, so many deformations and deviations occurred that I had to stop and think and constantly remember Che and his premonition, his rejection of those methods for socialist construction. I think that what has happened in the socialist camp makes Che's economic thinking on the construction of socialism more timely than ever.

When the process of rectification was begun, I encouraged the printing of those books on Che and spread Che's economic thinking — but not for use as a manual, as something infallible, because you shouldn't take any school of political thought or the thinking of any theoretician or politician as something inflexible, as something dogmatic.

All my life, I've been the enemy of dogma. We should keep the thinking of the most illustrious politicians and of the most outstanding revolutionaries from becoming dogma, for all thinking corresponds to a given moment, circumstances, amount of information or experience. Thus, things that Lenin may have viewed at one time as correct formulas for dealing with a given circumstance may not be applicable in other, different circumstances or in different times.

The ideas of Marx, Engels, Lenin and Che aren't dogmas — they are brilliant samples of talent and of political, social and revolutionary vision created at a certain time. They are always applicable as long as you don't consider them immutable dogma; to do so would be to take them out of the scientific, political, revolutionary context and make them a matter of religion.

I tried to spread Che's ideas widely when we saw that the Soviet Union and the rest of the socialist camp were taking a different path, that led them farther and farther away from Che's thinking, when they were heading toward ever greater use of the categories and mechanisms of capitalism. In their efforts to improve socialism, they were using larger and larger amounts of the poison that was killing socialism. That's one of the causes of what happened in the socialist camp.

Glossary

Acevedo, Rogelio — served as member of Commission to Perpetuate the Memory of Commander Ernesto Guevara; currently member of Cuban Communist Party Central Committee.

Acuña, Juan Vitalio (Joaquín) (1925-1967) — veteran of Cuban revolutionary war; member of Cuban CP Central Committee; leading member of Guevara's detachment in Bolivia; after April 17, 1967, led column separated from main unit; killed in ambush, August 31, 1967.

Almeida, Juan (1927-) — participant in 1953 Moncada attack and imprisoned subsequently; *Granma* expeditionary and commander in Rebel Army; currently member of Central Committee and Political Bureau of Communist Party of Cuba; headed Commission to Perpetuate the Memory of Commander Ernesto Guevara.

Arbenz, Jacobo (1914-1971) — president of Guatemala, 1951-54; overthrown by CIA-backed coup in 1954.

Barrientos, René (1919-1969) — Bolivian general; a leader of November 1964 military coup; president from July 1966 until death in helicopter crash.

Batista, Fulgencio (1901-1973) — army sergeant who seized control of Cuban government in 1934; left office, 1944; led military coup in March 1952; dictator until January 1, 1959, when he fled Cuba.

Bunke, Tamara (Tania) (1937-1967) — born in Argentina and raised in German Democratic Republic; lived in Cuba 1961-64; went to Bolivia in 1964 to do advance work for guerrilla movement; incorporated into Guevara's column April 1967;

162

killed in ambush August 31, 1967.

Caamaño, Francisco (1932-1973) — colonel in Dominican Republic armed forces; central figure in April 1965 constitutional revolution, leading resistance to invading U.S. troops; subsequently went into exile in Cuba; led guerrilla expedition to Dominican Republic in 1973; captured shortly after and murdered by government troops.

Castro, Fidel (1926-) — born into a well-off landowning family, graduated from law school at the University of Havana. While at university he joined a student group against political corruption and was later a member of the Cuban People's Party (also known as the Orthodox Party) and became a leader of its left wing. In the same year he volunteered for an expedition to fight the Trujillo dictatorship in the Dominican Republic, although the expedition was subsequently unable to leave Cuba. As a student leader Castro went to Colombia to assist in the organization of a Latin American anti-imperialist student congress, and while there participated in the April 1948 popular revolt in Bogota. After the March 1952 coup by Fulgencio Batista, Castro began to organize a revolutionary grouping to initiate an armed insurrection against the dictatorship. He organized and led an unsuccessful atack on the Moncada army garrison in Santiago de Cuba on July 26, 1953. He and more than 25 others were captured and imprisoned, while more than 60 others were murdered by the army during and immediately after the assault. Castro's defense statement to the court was to be published as *History will absolve me*. Tens of thousands of copies of what was to become the program of the July 26 Movement were distributed. After a public campaign in support of their civil rights, Castro and the other prisoners were released in May 1955 after 22 months imprisonment. On July 7, 1955 he left for Mexico where he began to organize a guerrilla expedition to Cuba. On December 2, 1956, he and 81 others reached the Cuban coast aboard the cabin cruiser *Granma*. In the following two years Castro led the operations of the Rebel Army as well as functioning as the central leader of the July 26 Movement. After an initial setback, the guerrillas reorganized their forces and by late 1958 had successfully extended the revolutionary war from the Sierra Maestra mountains to the center of the island. Batista fled Cuba on January 1, 1959. Hundreds of thousands of Cubans responded to a call by Castro to launch a general strike against an attempt to impose a military government. Castro arrived in Havana on January 8, 1959. On February 13, 1959, he was named prime minister. In 1976 he became president of the Council of State and of the Council of Ministers. He has been first secretary of the Communist Party of Cuba since it was founded in 1965.

Castro, Raúl (1931-   ) — participant in Moncada attack and subsequently imprisoned; *Granma* expeditionary and commander in Rebel Army; minister of Revolutionary Armed Forces, 1959-present; vice-premier, 1959-76; in 1976 became first vice-president of Council of State and Council of Ministers; second secretary of Communist Party since 1965; brother of Fidel Castro.

Cienfuegos, Camilo (1932-1959) — *Granma* expeditionary; commander in Rebel Army; together with Guevara led march westward from Sierra Maestra to Las Villas Province; became Rebel Army chief of staff in January 1959; plane lost at sea on October 28, 1959.

Debray, Regis (1940-   ) — French journalist and supporter of Cuba; spent several weeks traveling with Guevara's guerrilla detachment; captured by Bolivian army when trying to leave; tried and sentenced to 30 years imprisonment; pardoned in 1970; later became prominent figure in French Socialist Party.

Granma — cabin cruiser used by revolutionaries to travel from Mexico to Cuba, November-December 1956; taken as name of daily newspaper of Communist Party of Cuba in 1965.

Guevara, Ernesto Che (1928-1967) — born in Rosario, Argentina. As a medical student in Buenos Aires and after graduating as a doctor, he traveled throughout Latin America. Living in Guatemala during 1954 — then under the elected government of Jacobo Arbenz — he became involved in political activity and witnessed the overthrow of that government in a CIA-backed coup. Forced to leave Guatemala, Guevara went to Mexico City. There he joined with exiled Cuban revolutionaries seeking to overthrow the regime of Fulgencio Batista. In July

1955 he met Fidel Castro and immediately enlisted in the guerrilla expedition being organized. He was given the nickname "Che" by the Cubans, a popular form of address in Argentina. From November 25 to December 2, 1956, Guevara sailed to Cuba aboard the cabin cruiser *Granma*. Originally the doctor, he became the first Rebel Army commander in July 1957. In September 1958, Guevara and Camilo Cienfuegos led guerrilla columns from the Sierra Maestra to the center of the island. In December 1958, Guevara led the Rebel Army forces to victory in the battle of Santa Clara. Following the triumph of the revolution on January 1, 1959, Guevara became a central leader of the new revolutionary government. In September 1959 he became head of the Department of Industry of the National Institute of Agrarian Reform. In November 1959 he was appointed as president of the National Bank of Cuba. In February 1961 he became the minister of industry. Guevara was also a leading representative of Cuba at many world forums, heading numerous delegations. In 1964 he spoke on behalf of Cuba at the United Nations. In 1965 Guevara left Cuba to directly participate in revolutionary struggles in Africa and Latin America. He spent several months in the Congo in Africa, returning to Cuba in December 1965. In November 1966 he arrived in Bolivia, where he was to lead a guerrilla group fighting that country's military dictatorship. He was wounded and captured by U.S.-trained Bolivian counterinsurgency troops — being guided by CIA agents — on October 8, 1967. Che Guevara was murdered the following day.

Guevara, Moisés (1939-1967) — Bolivian miners' leader; split from Bolivian Communist Party and joined rival party led by Oscar Zamora; left that group and joined Guevara's guerrilla column; killed in ambush August 31, 1967.

Joaquín. See Acuña, Juan Vitalio.

July 26 Movement — founded in 1955 by Fidel Castro and other revolutionaries; leading organization in Cuban revolution; fused with two other groups in 1961 to form what would eventually become Communist Party of Cuba.

Kolle, Jorge — leader of Communist Party of Bolivia; replaced Monje as general secretary in December 1967.

Lumumba, Patrice (1925-1961) — founder and president of Congolese National Movement; first prime minister of Congo (now Zaire) after independence from Belgium in June 1960; overthrown and imprisoned three months later in proimperialist coup; murdered by captors in February 1961.

Maceo, Antonio (1845-1896) — prominent military leader and strategist in the three Cuban independence wars; opposed 1878 treaty that ended first war; led march from eastern to western ends of island in 1895-86; killed in battle.

March, Aleida (1934-   ) — member of July 26 Movement underground; joined Guevara's Rebel Army column; became Guevara's wife in 1959.

Marcos. See Sánchez, Antonio.

Martí, José (1853-1895) — Cuban national hero; noted poet, writer, speaker, and journalist; founded Cuban Revolutionary Party in 1892 to fight Spanish rule and oppose U.S. annexationist designs; launched 1895 independence war; killed in battle.

Massetti, Jorge Ricardo (1929-1964) — Argentinian journalist; traveled to Sierra Maestra in January 1958 and joined Rebel movement; founding director of Prensa Latina, Cuba's press service; killed while organizing guerrilla movement in Argentina.

Matos, Huber (1919-   ) — commander in Rebel Army; attempted to organize October 1959 counterrevolutionary rebellion in Camagüey Province; arrested and imprisoned until 1979; now living in United States.

Mella, Julio Antonio (1903-1929) — leader of university reform movement in 1923; a founding leader of first Communist Party of Cuba in 1925; assassinated in Mexico by agents of Cuba's Machado dictatorship.

Moncada — former army garrison in Santiago de Cuba; attacked by Fidel Castro and over 100 revolutionaries on July 26, 1953; dozens of captured revolutionaries subsequently assassinated; Castro captured and imprisoned; has come to mark the beginning of revolutionary struggle against Batista.

Monje, Mario — general secretary of Bolivian Communist Party until December 1967; subsequently leading member of its

Central Committee.

National Institute of Agrarian Reform (INRA) — created May 17, 1959, to implement agrarian reform law; coordinated Cuban factory production until formation of Ministry of Industry in 1961; dissolved in 1976.

Ovando, Alfredo (1918-   ) — Bolivian general; helped lead November 1964 coup; Bolivian president, 1965-66, 1969-70; as army commander led military campaign against Guevara.

Peredo, Coco (1938-1967) — member of Bolivian Communist Party; joined Guevara's guerrilla detachment; killed September 26, 1967.

Peredo, Inti (1937-1969) — member of Bolivian Communist Party; survivor of Guevara's guerrilla detachment and continued guerrilla activity; assassinated in La Paz, September 9, 1969.

Playa Girón — beach near Bay of Pigs where last of 1,500 mercenary troops invading Cuba surrendered April 19, 1961; Cubans use this name to refer to entire battle.

Prado, Gary — Bolivian captain; head of Ranger unit that captured Guevara; later became general; author of *Como capturé al Che* (How I captured Che).

Rebel Army — armed force of July 26 Movement in revolutionary war against Batista; became Revolutionary Armed Forces in 1959.

Reyes, Simón — leader of Bolivian Communist Party and mine workers union; later became general secretary of party.

Rojas, Honorato — Bolivian peasant visited by guerrillas; led army to ambush site where Joaquín's group was annihilated; executed in reprisal by guerrillas in 1969.

Sánchez, Antonio (Marcos) (1927-1967) — veteran of Cuban revolutionary war and member of Central Committee of Cuban Communist Party; member of Guevara's guerrilla detachment in Bolivia; killed in ambush June 2, 1967.

Soumialot, Gaston-Emile — minister of defense and head of army in Congo People's Republic, rebel government set up 1964 in Stanleyville by followers of Lumumba; defeated by Belgian troops and foreign mercenaries; assisted by Guevara and Cuban internationalist fighters.

Tamara (Tania). See Bunke, Tamara.

Valdés, Ramiro (1932-   ) — participant in Moncada attack and *Granma* expedition; commander in Rebel Army; currently a member of Communist Party Central Committee.

Zamora, Oscar — led split from Bolivian Communist Party in 1965; general secretary of rival Communist Party.

Zayas, Alfonso — served as member of Commission to Perpetuate the Memory of Commander Ernesto Guevara; member of Cuban Communist Party Central Committee for many years.

Zenteno, Joaquín — Bolivian colonel; commander of Eighth Division that fought Guevara's detachment.

AFROCUBA
An anthology of Cuban writing on race, politics and culture
Edited by Pedro Pérez Sarduy and Jean Stubbs
ISBN 1-875284-41-9

CUBA: TALKING ABOUT REVOLUTION
New, expanded edition
Conversations with Juan Antonio Blanco by Medea Benjamin

FIDEL AND RELIGION
A conversation with Frei Betto
ISBN 1-875284-05-2

THE FERTILE PRISON
Fidel Castro in Batista's jails
by Mario Mencía
ISBN 1-875284-08-7

CUBA AT THE CROSSROADS
by Fidel Castro
ISBN 1-875284-94-X

PRIEST AND PARTISAN
A South African journey
by Michael Worsnip
ISBN 1-875284-96-6

SLOVO — The unfinished autobiography
ISBN 1-875284-95-8

OCEAN PRESS DISTRIBUTORS:

Australia and New Zealand: Astam Books, 57 John St, Leichhardt, NSW 2040
Britain and Europe: Central Books, 99 Wallis Road, London E9 5LN, Britain
Canada: Marginal Distribution, 277 George St. N., Unit 102, Peterborough,
Ontario K9J 3G9, Canada
Cuba and Latin America: Ocean Press, Apartado 686, C.P. 11300, Havana
South Africa: Phambili Agencies, PO Box 28680, Kensington Gardens, 2101
*United States:*The Talman Company, 131 Spring Street, New York, NY 10012